Seeking a Revival Culture

Seeking a Revival Culture

Essays on Fortifying an Anemic Church

ALLEN M. BAKER III

RESOURCE *Publications* • Eugene, Oregon

SEEKING A REVIVAL CULTURE
Essays on Fortifying an Anemic Church

Resource Publishing
A Division of Wipf and Stock Publishers
199 W. 8th Ave., Suite 3
Eugene, OR 97401
www.wipfandstock.com

ISBN 13: 978-1-60608-524-0

Manufactured in the U.S.A.

All Scripture references, unless otherwise noted, are from the *New American Standard Bible*, The Lockman Foundation, 1977 edition, La Habra, California.

I dedicate this, my first book, to the love of my life, my dear wife,
the woman who has stood beside me in the good times and the bad.
I love you Wini.

An excellent wife, who can find?
For her worth is far above all jewels.

PROVERBS 31:10

Contents

Introduction

THE GREAT BURDEN OF my life, that which drives me in ministry more than anything else, is to see the church of our blessed Lord Jesus Christ rise up and become mighty like she has been so many times in the past. I have the privilege of preaching in other places in the United States and one thing has become very clear to me. The western church is in big trouble. Most pastors I know are terribly discouraged in their ministries. So are their people. The influx of immigrants from middle eastern countries that are predominantly Muslim, as well as Hispanic people who are historically Roman Catholic, along with our lack of power in reaching these people with the gospel; not to mention the secularization of our post-modern culture all are working to mitigate the church's effectiveness in the west. We are simply losing ground.

Pastors have been told that they can model their ministries after whoever the latest and hottest preacher is, and all will be well with them, that they can expect exponential growth in their churches. With few exceptions, this has not been their experience. They have attended the seminars and have read the latest books, but they have little to show for it. As a pastor I am troubled and heartbroken over the vastness of people's problems in today's world. I have been in the ministry nearly thirty years now and have never seen the number and depth of problems as today— everything from incest, child molestation, homosexuality, pornography, severe depression, suicide, divorce, wayward children, adultery, fornication, and more. All the pastors I know confirm my observations. The pastoral problems are epidemic. The Christian faith in our churches is woefully lacking. Our people are generally no different from those of the world.

Recently I was in East Africa preaching and was struck by a vivid illustration of the weakness of the American church. The indigenous church of this East African nation was thriving under African leadership. There was power, unity, conversions, and growth in holiness. Another younger denomination was struggling with division, lack of numerical growth and conversions, and a general sense of worldliness and powerlessness. When I asked the reason for the latter's weakness, I was told that we in the west have imported our anemia to the leaders of that denomination. I am grieved. In such circumstances we would be better not to send any of our western missionaries. They need Holy Spirit power, not our anemic, insipid, impotent brand of Christianity.

What are we to do? We need revival. We need a revival culture in the western church. We need, like Israel laboring under Egyptian bondage, to become intolerable of our circumstances. Israel cried out to the Lord when their slavery became intolerable to them. May God move us to divine discontent, to be dissatisfied with the status quo!

These essays, with minor additions and corrections, first appeared as part of my weekly devotional series called *Forget None of His Benefits* that is emailed weekly. Many have encouraged me over the years to have them published, and Wipf and Stock of Eugene, Oregon has graciously agreed to do so. I promise to give any profits from the sale of this book to world missions. My prayer is that these essays will move all of us to pursue Christ with the earnestness and zeal His life, death, and resurrection deserve.

Perhaps the best way to benefit from these essays is to read one per week (there are fifty-two of them), and ask God to show you your sin, to move you to repentance, to encourage you through the ministry of the Holy Spirit. I know many who use these devotionals as fodder for weekly discussion and prayer groups. I urge you to do the same. Gloria in excelsis Deo!

Ichabod

Ichabod. The glory has departed.

JOHN WINTHROP, WHILE STANDING on the bow of the *Arbella* in 1630, prior to his departure to the new world, gave the most important sermon in the second millennium, *A City on a Hill*.[1] In it Winthrop laid out the Puritan vision for the new world, that which has clearly served as the foundation for so much of what is good in our country, including our Protestant work ethic, the importance of education, and treating all people with honor and respect. The next generation provided us with Cotton Mather of Boston, a great preacher and theologian who was fluent in Latin, Greek, and Hebrew by the time he was ten, and who is the youngest to enter Harvard, having done so at the age of eleven. The following generation gave us the greatest philosopher and theologian in our history, Jonathan Edwards, whose writings are now more popular than ever. But then we began to see a change in the fabric of American Christianity. Charles Finney, a Presbyterian who dismissed the *Westminster Confession of Faith*, denied the doctrine of total inability, and consequently developed "new measures" that he used to urge conversion to Christ. Asahel Nettleton, also a Presbyterian (both were born in Connecticut), stood against Finney and his new measures, but Finney won a more popular following than Nettleton. Consequently Finney's theology has generally held sway over Nettleton's Old School Presbyterianism ever since.[2] By the middle of the nineteenth century we have on the scene the most famous man of the day, the son of Lyman Beecher, the brother of Harriett Beecher Stowe. I am referring to Henry Ward Beecher, a pastor from Brooklyn

1. Morgan, *The Puritan Dilemma*, 15.
2. For a very good overview of the Old School, New School Presbyterian debate, see Morton Smith's *Studies in Southern Presbyterian Theology*, published by P & R Publishers.

who became incredibly rich by pulpit, print, and platform (preaching, publishing novels, sermons, and newspapers, and lecturing all over the country). Beecher seemed to deny the most basic doctrines of the faith, and was said to look out any given Sunday on his congregation and find ten of his mistresses sitting there. But we have fallen even further in our own day with *Your Best Life Now* being one of the most popular Christian books in print.[3] We have fallen from a God-centered, Christ-exalting, Spirit-anointed, man-debasing theology to one that dethrones God and places man at the center of everything. The glory has departed. Only seventeen percent of Americans (whether they are Roman Catholics, mainline Protestants, or Evangelicals) are in church on any given weekend. Only eight percent are evangelical in our nation, and only one percent is evangelical in Connecticut where I live.

What are we to do? We must begin with God. More specifically I have in mind the necessity of beginning with the doctrine of God. He is holy, righteous, just, and will by no means leave the guilty unpunished. We must recapture the biblical doctrine of hell and eternal judgment. Most, even within evangelical churches, get nervous about this doctrine. They fear people will reject Christ if we speak too directly on the doctrine of hell. People have always rejected this doctrine. Such opposition is not new. God's judgment on the wicked is unavoidable and unutterable in its severity. Jesus spoke of hell as a place where the fire is never quenched and the worm never dies. He spoke of a lake of fire. He spoke of outer darkness where there is weeping and gnashing of teeth. We need to be clear on when this judgment will come. Paul says that due to our stubbornness and unrepentant heart we are storing up for ourselves wrath in the day of wrath and revelation of God who will render to every man according to his deeds (Romans 2:4ff). He told the Jews who were abusing the Thessalonians that they were filling up the measure or container of their sins, that God's wrath would come upon them to the utmost, (1 Thessalonians 2:16). God is patient with the impenitent, but there is a limit to it. When the measure of any sinner's sins reaches the top of the container, then death and judgment are soon to follow. And why does God promise an unavoidable and intolerable judgment? For Him to refuse would be to deny His character. He is holy, just, sovereign, good, wise, and gracious (see Isaiah 6, Psalm 103, Psalm 145). The punishment must

---

3. Joel Osteen wrote *Your Best Life Now* in 2004, published by Warner Faith Publications.

fit the crime. A poor woman who steals bread from a rich man to feed her starving children is not as guilty as a young man who steals from his rich father to feed his drug habit. Both are wrong, though the latter is more wrong. Why? Because the crime of stealing from one's father to feed a drug habit is far worse than the first scenario. Your sin is against the great, holy, and sovereign God. You have committed high treason against the King of Kings and Lord of Lords. God, therefore, is perfectly just in punishing all unredeemed sinners with eternal hell.

Here's my question to you. Do you really believe all this? Most of you will say you believe it, but do you really? If these things are true, then should we not be all about warning people to flee from the coming wrath of God and to believe on the Lord Jesus Christ? Can there be anything more important than to offer people the only means of reconciliation, the only means of escaping a fiery, eternal hell? I trace the problems in our country (whether they are related to race, materialism, family disintegration, or debauchery) to the decline of biblical preaching in our churches. This problem is not new. It has been with us as early as the 1750's when preachers began moving away from a God-centered, Christ-exalting, man-debasing theology to one increasingly pregnant with man's transcendence and self-reliance. Preachers have grown soft on the doctrine of God's sovereignty, instead embracing a false gospel of man's autonomy. Preachers have embraced Arminianism, which teaches that man holds the last card, that he decides whether or not he will become a Christian. Preachers have forgotten the basic truth that Christ will build His church, and have thus moved toward manipulation and persuasion to draw a crowd, slowly but surely moving away from the S(in) and H(ell) words. The church therefore is weak, tepid, worldly, powerless to stand against the onslaught of post-modernity. We are like a de-fanged lion.

I am deeply grieved over the condition of the church in America. What are we to do? We must pray, asking God the Holy Spirit to come upon preachers, granting them boldness to preach the doctrines of God's holiness, Christ's atoning death, and the necessity of the new birth. These same preachers must turn away from sin, all the while abiding in Christ, never forgetting their dependence upon the Spirit for everything. They must be sensitive to the Spirit's indwelling and leading by keeping short accounts with God, repenting quickly and humbly when their sin is revealed to them. They must remember they will stand before the judgment seat of Christ and be judged according to their deeds. They will give an account of their labors for Christ. And they must daily surrender everything to Jesus, not holding back like Achan did with the spoil. They must be willing to spend and be spent for the sake of the gospel. They must be willing to be fools for Christ's sake.

They must be willing to suffer reproach and false accusations. They must die to self. We must all die to self and seek the glory of God in the face of Christ.

Confronting Our Neo-Pagan World

. . . to the saints who are at Ephesus, and who are faithful in Christ Jesus.

EPHESIANS 1:1

*P*ANEM ET CIRCENCES, BREAD and circuses. This phrase was coined by the Roman satirical writer Juvenal to describe the ethos of Roman life in the first century A.D. Rome then had a population of one and one-half million and was the greatest city in the world, replete with prosperity beyond comprehension. The people had plenty to eat, and they were addicted to entertainment and the craze of sport. The Roman coliseum was only slightly smaller than the modern day Los Angeles Coliseum. The Circus Maximus sat over three hundred thousand sports enthusiasts. Nero wore his robes of opulence only once, and then discarded them. Caligula, who had a favorite horse he wanted to make a Senator, shod his horse in gold shoes. The pagan worship of Isis and Diana was rampant throughout the empire, and in Rome people worshipped the goddess of a thousand names, Cybele.[4]

Are we really much different today? I remember the Contract with America in the 1994 Congressional and Senatorial elections, sweeping a majority of Republicans into both the House and the Senate, and many Christians were ecstatic, thinking this event would turn the tide of godlessness in our culture. Did it? I remember not being impressed by the results of the election because what drove the voting was money, economics. The Republicans were not interested in social or ethical issues. People get serious about voting certain people out of office when it hits their check book and stock portfolios, but social issues rarely cause the same upheaval in the political process.

Indeed, as the Fifth Dimension once sang, we are now in the dawning of the Age of Aquarius. The Age of Pisces (the fish, the ancient sym-

---

4. Jones, *Capturing the Pagan Mind*, 6ff.

bol for Christianity) has given way to Aquarius, the sign of paganism. The evangelical church in America is in big trouble. We simply are not growing, and haven't been since *Time* magazine declared 1976 the "Year of the Evangelical."

What are we to do? First, I suggest you read prayerfully Peter Jones' book *Capturing the Pagan Mind*[5], and work to apply Pauline theology to our culture, to confront our culture with the truth of God as it is in Jesus. Paul's Roman culture was very similar to ours. Why then should we not use his approach to ministry? The very foundation of this approach must be a firmly held conviction of the sovereignty of God, that man is not sovereign, that man does not call the shots, that God is in heaven and does as He pleases. Why is this concept important? Well, if we believe man has something left deep in the core of his being that causes him to seek God, then we will use whatever means possible to win him, and to convince him. As recent history shows, we fall into all manner of folly including drama, cheesy worship services, and psychotherapeutic preaching. Really now, where has this approach gotten us? Are we transforming our culture? Or are we merely encouraging people to continue in their self-absorption and worldliness?

Second, it means that we must be clear on who we are. Paul says three things about us in Ephesians 1:1 that are absolutely essential. First, we must understand experientially that we are saints, second that we are called to faithfulness, and third that we are in Christ Jesus. You have been set apart by God through His grace. A radical transformation has occurred in you if you are a believer. Everything about you has changed. You are not your own. You belong body and soul to your blessed Savior Christ Jesus who redeemed you by His blood. You have a new heart, which now hates sin and loves righteousness. You needed a heart transplant, and Jesus was the donor. He gave you His heart. Never forget it; believe it; live it out daily. To be faithful means that you believe certain things about God, Christ, the Holy Spirit, yourself, the nature of the world, and eternity. It means you embrace, contend for, and defend this Biblical truth without compromise in a neo-pagan world. It means you put away childish things, that you are done with lesser things. It means you purpose to live in obedience to the commands of God's word. And you are in Christ Jesus, which means you are in a vital, organic, and mystical union with Jesus. He

5. Ibid.

is the vine, and we are the branches. Apart from Him we can do nothing, but attached to Him we can and will bring forth much fruit. You must obey God in all things, including loving Him with all your heart and your neighbor as yourself. You must love your wife or submit to your husband or train children in godly living. You must rejoice with those who rejoice and weep for those who weep. You must, but you cannot. You cannot love God and your fellow man or carry out any other command from God. You consequently thirst for righteousness, being like a tree planted by a stream of water that yields its fruit in its season. Abide in Jesus by faith. This is your only hope.

We attack our neo-pagan world by first and foremost holding onto the sovereignty of God and our identity in Jesus. Thus you should never be given to despair, anxiety, or hopelessness about the world or the state of the church. We must begin here. Change your thinking Christian, and let it grip you. Let it take possession of your heart.

What We Learned from Harvard's Fall

Be on guard . . . to shepherd the church of God . . . after my departure savage wolves will come in among you, not sparing the flock.

ACTS 20:28–29

I N 1636, ONLY SIX years after landing at Boston, the Massachusetts Bay Colony received a charter from the crown of England to establish a college to train men for the gospel ministry. The first great benefactor of the college, John Harvard, left half his estate and his library of four hundred books to establish the college across the Charles River in Cambridge. From the very beginning Harvard combined God-centered, Christ-exalting theology with scholarship, requiring all men, prior to their entrance to be able to read and understand the great Latin classics and to be able to decline perfectly the New Testament Greek noun and verb paradigms.[6]

Things generally progressed well at Harvard for the first sixty years or so, but finally a change in mood became noticeable. Students, faculty, and the general public clamored for a more open, tolerant, and catholic (universal) spirit, not being so narrow in the Puritan theology that permeated the ethos of Harvard. This shift gave way rather quickly to a change in methods. Thomas and William Brattle, two well-to-do brothers, established the Brattle Street Church that moved away from long expositions of Scripture in preaching to ritual and mere reading of the Bible in the worship services. They also discontinued the Puritan practice of requiring *conversion narratives* in order to become members of the church (what we call today a testimony of one's Christian experience). Eventually a change in morals was noticeable among the students at Harvard who were preparing for the ministry in the Congregational Church. Already the Congregationalists in Connecticut were concerned about the slide

---

6. David Beale, "Lessons Learned From the Fall of Harvard", study paper, Bob Jones University.

into modernity at Harvard, and with the help of Increase Mather established Yale in 1701. In 1725 one complained that the students were given "to drinking frolics, poultry stealing, profane cursing, bringing live snakes and rum into their residences, and given to scandalous and shameful behavior."[7] When George Whitefield preached there in 1740 he was stunned by the carelessness of the students concerning their souls and their lack of experiential holiness. In 1776 the students at Harvard wrote the President, Samuel Langdon, demanding his resignation, saying, "Sir as a man of piety we venerate you, but as a President, we despise you." An earlier president quietly went away, having made his house maid pregnant.

And finally—as so often happens in churches, schools, business, and families—a change in mood, that gives way to a change in methods, that gives way to a change in morals, eventually gives way to a change in message. In other words, a change in morality always dictates a change in theology in order to justify behavior. By 1800 Harvard was struggling to maintain the old Puritan, Calvinistic theology. Then President Joseph Willard died in 1803. The very next year, the Chair of the Hollis School of Divinity, David Tappan, someone who was committed to the old theology, also died. In his place the Board of Directors appointed Henry Ware, a Unitarian. The ensuing Unitarianism of Harvard has had a profound and lasting effect on our nation, in ways that most people cannot comprehend. This denial of biblical faith is the genesis of the public school movement of Horace Mann and John Dewey, both of whom were church-going Unitarians.

We are all prone toward spiritual declension (from the Latin word *declinatio*[8]), a falling away from biblical piety. Our mood may change first, thinking that vigilance in what we watch or listen to is not really that important. Since we are under grace, we may wrongly assume that oversight of what our children watch, and whom they befriend is not really a concern. The next thing that goes is our methods. We compromise and watch television programming we would never have considered ten years ago. We may depart slightly from the norm at work by putting a different spin on a report or product because, after all, our company needs a better bottom line for this quarter. And then our morals change. We justify lying by fudging our expense reports or income taxes or by complimenting ourselves on how we

7. Ibid.

8. From the Latin *declinatio*, a going down. Thus Latin or Greek declensions are a going down from the nominative to the accusative cases. I am indebted to Brian McCarthy for this insight.

do not look at internet pornography, but see nothing wrong with perusing websites of the *SI* swimsuit or *Victoria Secret* models. By then, of course, knowingly or unknowingly we alter our message. Now we may champion doctrines like eternal security (once saved always saved) while ignoring sober warnings like Hebrews 10:26ff, "For if we go on sinning willfully after receiving the knowledge of the truth, there no longer remains a sacrifice for sins, but a certain terrifying expectation of judgment and the fury of a fire which will consume the adversaries." We tend to ignore the statements of perseverance from Revelation 2 and 3, "To him who overcomes, I will grant to eat of the tree of life ... he who overcomes shall not be hurt by the second death ... to him who overcomes I will give some of the hidden manna ... to him who overcomes, and he who keeps My deeds until the end, to him I will give authority over the nations ..."

These warnings to persevere are why Elders or church officers are so vital to your spiritual life. They are to keep watch over your souls. A revival culture can develop when they point out tendencies toward spiritual declension and warn you of them, calling you to repentance if you succumb to the harlot. The harlot of Revelation is the opposite of the church, the bride of Christ. She seduces believers away from simplicity and purity of devotion to Christ, causing them to find their joy in money, things, hobbies, children, etc. Are you cold in heart? Have you lost your appetite for public and private worship? When is the last time you felt God's presence powerfully working in you in public and private worship? By the way, this has nothing to do with the form of worship—contemporary, blended, or traditional. Are you moved by the worship of God? Are you careless with your sins? Has your mood, methods, morals, and message changed? Are you like the old Harvard that began so well but has become so debauched? Repent and do the deeds that you did at first or else Christ will come to you and remove your lamp stand (a Christ-centered church and preacher) out of its place. The gospel has left the Middle East, North Africa, and Europe. America is not far behind.

Pray for your pastor and church officers, that they will take seriously their responsibilities as Christ's under shepherds, and submit to their loving, humble, and gracious oversight.

Election

*Just as He chose us in Him before the foundation of the world, that we
should be holy and blameless before Him in love,*

EPHESIANS 1:4

YOUNG MARY STUART SET foot on Scottish soil in August 1561 to become the Queen of Scotland. She was a young, beautiful, and seductive woman who was accustomed to getting her way. She was incensed that Scotland had forsaken Roman Catholicism for the Reformation led by John Knox. Her first order of business, on the first Sunday she was in Edinburgh, was to have the Mass at Holyrood Castle. Just up the street at the St. Giles Presbyterian Church, Knox railed against her in his sermon, calling her a whore and warning of the catastrophe of going back to Roman Catholicism. The Reformation by 1561 was firmly entrenched in Scotland, and the people were enjoying their liberty and increased economic empowerment. Queen Mary knew, in order to win back Scotland to her cause, she must neutralize Knox.[9] She summoned him to her castle and sought to flatter him. Many a man had wilted under her charm, but Knox was an old man by this time, and had suffered far too much to be seduced by her. He had spent nineteen months as a galley slave on a French ship in his mid forties. He stood resolute against her flattery, and when that did not work she sought to intimidate him. Bad idea! Knox was bold beyond comprehension, and there was no way he would be intimidated by any human being. If Knox had given in to her seduction, then the Reformation would have been lost to Scotland. Hundreds would have died, and the Scottish Enlightenment that brought so much to our modern world would have stalled and finally died.[10]

9. John Knox, *The Reformation in Scotland*, 271.

10. For a fascinating study you may wish to read *How the Scots Invented the Modern World* by Arthur Herman.

What, you may ask, has this history to do with the doctrine of election? It illustrates a powerful application of the doctrine. First, what does Paul mean, "just as He chose us in Him before the foundation of the world"? Here and also in Deuteronomy 7 and 10, John 6, and Romans 8 and 9 we are told that the sovereign God of grace, for His own praise and glory and not for anything He finds in us, chose a specific number of people out of all those in the world to be His. Furthermore, He did this before time, in eternity past. The Greek word translated "chosen" literally means called out of. This election is unconditional, meaning God did not look down the corridors of time to see if we would choose Him or if we would be faithful to Him. He chose us not based at all on anything we could offer Him. We are told on three occasions in Ephesians 1:4–14 that God's mighty work of election, predestination, adoption, and redemption is to the praise of the glory of His grace, according to the kind intention of His will.

Here's a practical application you can make to the doctrine of election—why are you a Christian? Why are your neighbors, your friends, or other family members not Christians while you are? Is it because you are smarter than they, more inclined toward faith, more moral? Not hardly. You are a Christian simply because God chose you to be one. He decided to bestow mercy upon you in eternity past. To put it another way, God in His foreknowledge has known you and loved you as long as He has existed, forever. Here's another application, drawn from my story of Knox and Queen Mary. I often tell the people in our church that due to these great doctrines of grace—the fact that God chose you in Christ, that He predestined you, that He adopted you into His family, that the Lord Jesus shed His blood for you—you can and should learn to argue from the greater down to the lesser. In other words, if God has done this mighty work in you, and if this is the most important issue in your life (and surely it is), then does it not naturally follow that God can and will take care of your lesser needs?

Perhaps the most vital and important reason that John Knox could be so bold, and so courageous was that he knew he belonged to Christ, that God had chosen him, that God had a purpose for his life, and that no matter what happened to him, he knew Christ was his and he was Christ's. When you know the love of the Father, when you know He has always loved you, when you know that He is sovereign in absolutely everything, that nothing escapes His notice, that He foreordains whatsoever comes to pass, and that no one can thwart His plans, then you can and should live with absolute calmness and peace: fearing no one, and falling to no one's intimidation or flattery. Knox did. By God's grace he cultivated a revival culture in Scotland, and we can too in our day. Do you believe this? Are you ready to seek God for it? This is the revival life the western church so desperately needs.

Predestination

He predestined us to adoption as sons through Jesus Christ to Himself,
according to the kind intention of His will.

EPHESIANS 1:5

JAMES ARMINIUS STUDIED IN Geneva under John Calvin's successor
Theodore Beza, and returned to his native Holland in 1581. The *Belgic Confession*, a confession of faith based on the Reformation doctrines then sweeping through Europe, was written in 1561 by Reformers in Belgium. It was quickly embraced by people in the Netherlands. It was written amidst atrocities committed by King Phillip II of Spain when anywhere from two thousand to one hundred thousand (depending on who one reads) were murdered. In 1581 the Reformed Church in the Netherlands embraced the *Heidelberg Catechism*, the most devotional of all the Reformed confessions of faith. It is in this context that Arminius was teaching and preaching, and many were suspect of his doctrine. When he was interviewed in 1601 to become a professor he was directly asked if his doctrine was consistent with the *Belgic Confession* and *Heidelberg Catechism*. He concurred, saying that he had not and would not teach anything contrary to both. Publicly he honored his word, but privately he was teaching a number of young men spurious doctrine. By 1609 the Reformed Church in the Netherlands brought charges against Arminius, but before he could be brought to trial, he died, probably of tuberculosis. A group of his disciples, called Remonstrants, took up his cause, and focused on five areas of disagreement. They denied (1) unconditional election, (2) the doctrine of original sin and consequent inability to choose to believe in Christ, (3) the atonement of Christ applied to the elect only, (4) the wooing of the Holy Spirit drawing people to Christ, and (5) the eternal security of the true believer. In 1619 a Synod in Dordrecht was called, summoning Reformed theologians from all over Europe to decide the case of the

Remonstrants. They came down on the side of heresy. We have had debate between Calvinism and Arminianism ever since.[11]

What does this controversy have to do with you and the doctrine of predestination? Paul builds on his statement in Ephesians 1:4 where he says that we were chosen by God before the foundation of the world. The ground of our election is the predestinating work of God, the fore-ordination of all things, meaning that God developed an overarching plan in eternity past. The center of that plan is the salvation of a specific number of people. He predestined the elect to adoption as His own sons and daughters. The idea of adoption as we know it today (that adopted children have the same rights, privileges, and obligations as natural children) was a concept foreign to the Hebrew mind of Paul's day. However it was quite common in the Roman world. Thus a true believer in Jesus Christ, as an adopted son or daughter of God, has an inheritance waiting for him in heaven that is far more glorious in its scope and magnitude than we can fathom.

Theologians have long debated how this doctrine plays itself out in people. What follows is not referring to chronology but more to the logic of order, how salvation works itself out in the mind of God. Arminianism believes in creation, and a partial fall (man is able to believe on Christ), but denies election, saying that people make a decision on their own free will to believe on Christ. Amyraldus, a Dutch theologian of the late seventeenth century, who believed in election, could not get past various passages that seem to teach that Jesus died for everyone. Consequently Amyraldus gave rise to what some call four point Calvinism. He denied particular redemption, that Jesus died only for the elect. The problem with Amyraldianism is that it pits the persons of the Godhead against each other—the Father chose a specific number of people, but Jesus died for everyone. Then there is Infralapsarianism (*infra* means after and *lapse* means fall, after the fall) that teaches creation, fall into sin, election, and then people becoming Christians at a specific time and place through the work of the Holy Spirit. The problem with this view is that it cannot explain fallen angels, like Lucifer, who must have fallen prior to man's fall into sin. How else would Adam have been tempted? Then there is Supralapsarianism (*supra* means before). In this view, in the mind of God, there was creation, election, then the fall into sin, and the application of

11. Vandergugten, "The Arminian Controversy and the Synod of Dort."

redemption where those drawn by the Spirit believe on Christ. Some are uncomfortable with this view because it seems to be cold and austere, suggesting that God capriciously chose some and condemned others, even before the fall into sin. I suggest that Supralapsarianism makes more sense, though Infralapsarianism is certainly an acceptable scheme of how salvation works its way out in the elect.[12] At the end of the day these issues cannot be discerned in the mind. They are heart matters. We may be confused, unable to resolve the tension between God's decree and human responsibility. However God is not confused. This tension is what we call the complementarity of truth. Jesus is both God and man. God elects and man decides for Christ. The Bible is God's word, but it is written by man. God hates sins, but God allows sin. God judges people in hell but God does not delight in the death of the wicked.

You may be saying, "Okay, so what? Why in the world is this important?" Because ideas matter. Theology drives all we do, whether we know it or not. To embrace Arminianism means one believes man has a small island of righteousness within him. It is to this island all evangelistic efforts must be focused. If this is true, then an evangelist is justified in using whatever means necessary to win a decision for Christ from those to whom he preaches. This theology has led to a plethora of false professions of faith and the cheesiness of much modern evangelicalism. It causes people to deny the need for earnest prayer and for the ministry of the Holy Spirit. It causes people to trust in plans, programs, and personalities. It causes many to go through life with a false sense of security, assuming that their decision for Christ many years before guarantees them eternal life.

But unless God chose you, unless the Lord Jesus Christ died for you, and unless the Holy Spirit regenerated you and gave you the grace to repent and believe the gospel, then you are still dead in your sins. Have you ever truly sensed your depravity and unsuitableness for salvation, and cast yourself unreservedly on the mercy of the Lord Jesus Christ? If not, then you are still dead in your sins. What are you to do? Repent and believe on Christ and bring forth fruits in keeping with repentance.

12. Reymond, *A New Systematic Theology of the Christian Faith*, 488–89.

Abundance

... which He lavished upon us in all wisdom and insight.

EPHESIANS 1:8

ROBERT LEWIS DABNEY WAS born in rural Virginia in 1820, and though he was not wealthy, he nonetheless was reared with a notion of the Old South aristocracy. As a young man he came to faith in the Lord Jesus Christ and attended Hamden Sydney College near Farmville, VA. Later, he received a seminary education at Union Theological Seminary, a Presbyterian Seminary near the Hamden Sydney campus. R. L. Dabney became the pastor of a small Presbyterian Church in Tinkling Spring, Virginia and saw a mighty revival sweep through his church and town, drawing a large number of people into Christ's kingdom. After a few years there, he became a professor of theology at Union Seminary and served as an officer for Thomas J. "Stonewall" Jackson during the War Between the States. The Confederacy's loss of that war devastated Dabney, and he had a very difficult time reconciling what he saw as the loss of Southern culture and theology in post-war years. Dabney was a wonderful theologian. In fact he wrote various essays that have come to sound quite prophetic in the late twentieth century and early twenty-first century. His essay on public education in the 1880's, where he predicted that public education would sooner or later forbid prayer and Bible reading in such schools, is a strong case in point.[13]

While Dabney was a great theologian, he had one glaring weakness. Sean Lucas of Covenant Seminary, in his biography on Dabney,[14] confirms what many have long suspected. Dabney was a racial bigot. To be sure, we ought to "cut him some slack" on the issue, realizing that most nineteenth century people, in both the North and South, viewed black people as

---

13. Dabney, *On Secular Education.*
14. Lucas, *Robert Lewis Dabney: A Southern Presbyterian Life.*

inferior; but there is no skirting the issue. In the post-war years Dabney's bitterness over the loss of Southern culture and aristocracy seemed to cut him off from the mainstream of theological discourse. The impact Dabney could have had was severely blunted by his anger, resentment, and bitterness over race and culture.

Interesting story, you may say, but what's the point? Here it is—if R. L. Dabney, one of our greatest theologians and a man of holiness and godliness, a man who knew well the doctrines of grace, could fall into such bitterness and resentment, then how much more so is that possible for you and me?

The Apostle Paul in Ephesians 1:7 has proclaimed the marvelous truth that in Christ we have redemption through His blood, the taking away of our trespasses according to the riches of His grace. Paul builds on that glorious proclamation by adding two phrases in verse 8—"which God lavished upon us in all wisdom and insight." Literally this grace He super abounded to us. It is an over abundance, overwhelming, over-the-top undeserved favor by God through the Lord Jesus Christ. The second phrase has to do with God super abounding this grace in all wisdom and insight. Conservative biblical commentators are divided on where to put this phrase.[15] Does it make more sense with "which He lavished upon us" or does it go better with verse 9, "He made known to us." It seems option one is best, for it is a foregone conclusion that God has all wisdom and in-sight. We don't need to be told that. Rather this grace that super abounded to us gives us wisdom and insight, knowledge with application, the ability to work out the knowledge of God we possess.

At least it ought to do so. Dabney knew very well the riches of God's grace. He taught and believed the doctrines of election, predestination, adoption, and redemption. He championed such doctrines. But there was this one area of his life where he failed to apply what he knew. He could have used more wisdom and insight.

How, in your own life, are you like R. L. Dabney? You know theologi-cally and biblically the riches of God's grace to you, but perhaps you are filled with racial pride or bigotry. Maybe you look with disgust on the immigrants in your community. Maybe you hold in contempt those of the hip hop culture. I am not saying that you must celebrate their culture. I am simply asking, are you bigoted? Are you a racist? And then we can move

15. For more on this debate see John Calvin, William Hendriksen, R.C.H. Lenski, and Peter O'Brien in their excellent Commentaries on Paul's Epistle to the Ephesians.

onto other issues. Is your life characterized by fear of people, anger or bitterness, worry? Are you slowly finding yourself put to the side because people simply do not enjoy being around you?

May God show you the blind spots in your own life! Yes, we rejoice over the super- abundant, over-the-top-grace but will you ask God to give you the wisdom and insight to more readily and practically apply what you already know? This wisdom and insight is the essence of the revival culture we so desperately need.

Mystery

*He made known to us the mystery of His will, according to His kind
intention which He purposed in Him.*

EPHESIANS 1:9

AUGUSTINE WAS BORN IN November 354 A.D. in Hippo, in North
Africa. His father's name was Patricius, and he was a pagan. His
mother was named Monica, and she was a believer. At the age of nineteen,
Augustine found a copy of Cicero's *Hortensius* and began a long search
for wisdom. At the age of twenty he embraced Manicheaism, a philosophy
that pursues ancient Zoroastrianism, Gnostic Christianity, and paganism,
and teaches that equal forces of good and evil are pitted against each
other in the world. When he was twenty-one Augustine became a teacher
of rhetoric, what we today would call today public speech and debate,
and was soon known as a great orator. He moved to Rome when he was
twenty-nine to further his career, and a year later ended up in Milan.
He studied the Christian faith under Ambrose, the Bishop of Milan. He
was still seeking wisdom a year later when he claimed to have a Platonic
ecstatic experience. Augustine was given over to sexual promiscuity and
debauchery, and had many mistresses. During all these years, his mother
Monica faithfully prayed for his salvation. Finally, Augustine was in a state
of great conflict. He believed Christianity was true, but he loved his licen-
tious lifestyle, and he knew that conversion to Christ would mean the end
of his debauchery. He was in a garden one day with his friend Alypius
when he asked to be by himself. He sat down on a bench and heard a child
saying over and over, "Tolle lege, tolle lege," This phrase meant, "Take up
and read, take up and read." Augustine saw a copy of Paul's epistle to the
Romans and opened it, reading the first passage he saw, "Let us behave
properly as in the day, putting aside all carousing and drunkenness, sexual
promiscuity and sensuality, jealousy and strife; and put on the Lord Jesus
Christ and make no provision for the flesh in regard to its lusts," (Romans

13:13–14). At that very moment Augustine saw his sin, repented, and believed on the Lord Jesus Christ. God the Holy Spirit utterly transformed Augustine from the inside out. He was wondrously converted and five years later became a pastor. Eventually he became a Bishop, and led the way against the heretic Pelagius, who denied original sin.[16]

All the years of searching for wisdom finally resulted in the mystery of the gospel being revealed to Augustine. Paul the Apostle in Ephesians 1:9 is speaking of this mystery. Jesus speaks of "the mystery of the kingdom" in Matthew 13:11. In Matthew 11:25, Jesus says, "Father I thank You that you have hidden these things from the wise and intelligent and have revealed them to babes." Paul speaks of this mystery in many places, (see Ephesians 3:2ff, 6:19, 1 Corinthians 2:6ff, Romans 11:25, 16:25, Colossians 1:27, 4:3). A mystery is something once concealed but later revealed. The Old Testament spoke of Christ but in types and shadows. The advent of Christ made the gospel clear. Paul is saying in Ephesians 1:9 that we ought to celebrate the revelation of the mystery of the gospel. The simple truth is this—if you are a believer in the Lord Jesus Christ, then the mystery of the gospel has been made clear to you. God has opened your eyes and ears. He has enabled you to repent and believe. There are, of course, other mysteries in the Bible, doctrines like the Trinity and the hypostatic union (how the two natures of Christ can be in one person), but Paul is speaking here of the mystery of the gospel made known to us for salvation by the work of the Holy Spirit.

Know this—the gospel continues to be, to those without eyes to see or ears to hear, utter and complete foolishness, (see 1 Corinthians 1:18, 2:14). Why? Theologians speak of the fall into sin putting us into a state of corruption, *status corruptionis*. This fall has rendered us *non posse, non peccare*, not possible not to sin. This corruption had produced in all of us the noetic (from the Greek word *nous*, which means mind) effects of sin. Our minds are so adversely affected by the fall that we cannot understand the gospel of Christ. It is foolishness to us. Here's an application for all church leaders—if this is true, then why compromise the gospel message? Why water it down? Why hint at the possibility of other ways to God? Why flatter people by refusing to tell them how corrupt they are, how sinful they are? Why stay away from the *H* word (the doctrine of hell)? The natural man, the unconverted, sees the gospel as foolishness. Of course he

16. Piper, *The Legacy of Sovereign Joy: God's Triumphant Grace in the Lives of Augustine, Luther, and Calvin*, 60.

does not believe it. The Holy Spirit must call him, regenerate him. Then and only then are his eyes and ears opened.

And here's a personal application—if you are a believer, remember that you had nothing to do with it. God has revealed the mystery to you. He has opened your eyes and ears so that you may rejoice in being called a sinner and in trusting the sufficiency of Christ on the cross.

And here is another practical application—put away your former poverty and live out your privileges, responsibilities, and securities. The old man, the old you, is dead (Romans 6:1–5), what you were before you became a Christian. Don't go back to the way you lived formerly. How stupid would it be for a wealthy man coming out of poverty to go back to that lifestyle! Instead live out your privileges. You can start by meditating on your adoption, your access to the Father, and the comforting fact of the Spirit and the Son are interceding for you, (see Romans 8:14ff). But you also need to live out your responsibilities. How about Romans 12:1ff, where you are commanded to offer yourselves as living sacrifices to God; where you are told to love one another, to forgive one another, to show kindness to one another, where you are called to live authentic lives before a watching world. And finally you need to live out your securities. Oh, there is so much in Scripture about this! Consider Isaiah 25:1, 43:1–3, 45:6ff, 46: 8ff, 40:27ff.

Will you bow in awe and wonder at God revealing to you the mystery of redemption? God in His sheer mercy has opened your eyes to see what so many cannot see. To whom much is given, much is required. Will you not live out your privileges, responsibilities, and securities in covenantal faithfulness? Will you not pour out your life for the progress of the gospel in your community and beyond? This progress is true revival living. It is Acts 2 Christianity.

Foreordination

In Him also we have obtained an inheritance, having been predestined according to His purpose who works all things after the counsel of His will.

EPHESIANS 1:11

JOHN OWEN, THE GREATEST of the Puritan theologians was born in 1616, the year William Shakespeare died and four years before the Pilgrims landed in Massachusetts. He was a brilliant theologian who wrote profound and helpful books that many still feast upon today. He served with Oliver Cromwell, The Lord Protector of England, during the cessation of kingly rule in England. Owen preached numerous times in Parliament, and was a major contributor at the Westminster Assembly in 1643 and onward. But Owen's public life is not what I want to stress here. He was married for thirty-one years and his wife blessed him with eleven children, ten of whom died in infancy and one as a young adult. His wife died five years before he did. How could Owen possibly live with a sense of peace, joy, and fervency for Christ in the midst of untold tragedy? It is true that death was very much a day to day reality for people in the seventeenth century, and families commonly experienced infant mortality. But eleven children? This number is truly remarkable. That's simply staggering. How was Owen able to weather such storms?[17]

Ephesians 1:11 gives us an insight. Paul, in verse 10, is presenting an overarching plan or purpose for all things, saying that Christ Jesus is the household manager as it were (*oikos, nomos,* our word *economics*) , given responsibility by the Father to direct and dispose all things for His glory. He goes on to say that Christ Jesus will sum up again, make all things right on that great day of His return. Now Paul deals with present realities. Every English translation of the Bible I have consulted translates this

---

17. Piper, *Contending for Our All: Defending Truth and Treasuring Christ in the Lives of Athanasius, John Owen, and J. Gresham Machen,* 87ff.

verse as inheritance or heritage, "In Him we have obtained an inheritance, a heritage." Certainly it is a glorious truth that we have an inheritance from the God, that we are heirs of God and fellow heirs with Christ; but I suggest "inheritance" is not what Paul has in view here. The Greek word is our root word for *lot*. In Joshua we read of how God directed Joshua to allot portions of land to the twelve tribes of Israel. It seems to me that a more accurate translation of this verse is, "in whom we also were made to receive a lot, this lot being foreordained or predestinated according to God's purpose, who continually works or energizes all things after His deliberate, well intentioned will." This means that you have a *lot* from God. Whatever your life situation is—marriage, children, health, money, you name it—this is God's lot for you. Furthermore, this lot has been foreordained, predestined by God, (see Romans 8:29–30, Isaiah 14:27, Daniel 4:34–35). God has planned it from eternity past. This plan is not bad luck, chance, or a matter of being at the wrong place at the wrong time. It is precisely what God had in mind for you and your loved ones. Furthermore, God is not merely one who set this in motion in eternity past and sits back and watches it unfold in today's world. He continually works in and through you to accomplish His well intentioned, gracious, most wise will for your life.

It is clear that the doctrine of foreordination, that God plans everything that happens in eternity past, is meant to evoke praise from us. After developing this doctrine in great detail in Romans 9–11, Paul says, "O the depths of the riches, both of the wisdom and knowledge of God! How unsearchable are His judgments and unfathomable His ways!" Praise and adoration is the order of the day for those who understand and embrace this doctrine. It also follows that the doctrine of providence is vital to our living with peace and security in the world. In Matthew 10:29–30, Jesus says, "Are not two sparrows sold for a cent? And yet not one of them will fall to the ground apart from your Father. But the very hairs of your head are numbered." And in Paul's sermon on Mars Hill he says, "And God made from one every nation of mankind on all the face of the earth, having determined their appointed times and the boundaries of their habitation," (Acts 17:26). In other words, God planned the nation in which you would be born, who your parents and siblings would be, and the century in which you would be born. He planned everything, and He directs, or carries out everything in your life.

I know what you are thinking—that sounds like we are not necessary, that we are merely robots with no freedom, no decision making power. Theologians refer to this as concurrence. God foreordains everything that comes to pass, but these things work themselves out in a real world where we make decisions everyday that impact our world, decisions for which we are directly responsible. The classic text on this is Acts 2:23 where Peter, preaching on the day of Pentecost says, "This Man, delivered up by the predetermined plan and foreknowledge of God, you nailed to a cross by the hands of godless men and put Him to death." There we find both God's foreordination and man's human responsibility. At the end of the day we must simply confess this to be one of many mysteries in the Bible, one of His complementarities of truth.

What does foreknowledge mean practically for you? This doctrine means three things. First, learn that God's plan for your life is not misery or calamity. His plan is for your welfare. It has a future and a hope, (see Jeremiah 29:11). I am not saying you do not experience misery or calamity. I am saying that God works all things together for good to those who love Him, to those who are called according to His purpose. Are you focusing on your calamity, not seeing the good the infinitely wise and gracious God is bringing or will bring to your life? Second, learn to see God in the details of your earthly journey. Joseph finally came to understand this truth after the turmoil of his brothers' abuse. He said to them, "You meant it for evil, but God meant it for good," Genesis 50:20. I am not saying you do not experience sorrow and confusion. I am saying you must learn to see God in the details, to trust Him, and to wait on Him. And third, learn to wait until that great day when God will make all things clear to you, (see 1 Corinthians 2:9). When you enter the glorious presence of our exalted mediator, the Lord Jesus Christ, then all the confusion, the sorrow, the misery and calamity, the injustice in your life will all make sense to you. You will see how the sovereign, gracious, all wise God of predestination, foreordaining providence, was behind everything and you will be able to say, "This was very good for my soul."

Pre-hoping in Christ

*. . . to the end that we who were the first to hope in Christ
should be to the praise of His glory.*

EPHESIANS 1:12

A THANASIUS WAS BORN IN Alexandria, Egypt in 298 A.D., converted
to Christ as a young man and was made Bishop of Alexandria at the
age of thirty, in 328 A.D. As John Piper notes in his brief biography of
Athanasius, the people of Egypt viewed him as their Bishop for forty-five
years until his death at the age of seventy-five. The Roman authorities
exiled Athanasius five times for a total of seventeen of those forty-five
years as Bishop, but throughout his absence the people still trusted him
and honored him. What was it that brought such hatred and opposition
to Athanasius? In 319 A.D. a priest named Arius said that if Jesus is God's
Son then He must have had a beginning. Some within the church immediately saw where such thinking would take people concerning the Trinity
and the person of Jesus Christ. If Jesus were created, then He must be less
than God; and if He is less than God, then the Trinity must be a corrupt
concept. This view finds expression today in the heresies of the Jehovah's
Witnesses and Mormons who both deny the deity of Christ. Constantine,
the Emperor of Rome (who set up the reign of his kingdom in Byzantium,
then called Constantinople, modern day Istanbul, Turkey) was concerned
about the political upheaval this controversy was causing in his kingdom
and summoned the leading theologians in the church to clear up the
matter. The result was the Nicene Creed of 325 A.D., still used today by
millions of Christians around the world as an orthodox statement of the
Trinity and deity of Christ. In part it says, "I believe . . . And in one Lord
Jesus Christ, the only begotten Son of God, begotten of the Father before

all worlds, God of God, Light of Light, very God of very God, begotten, not made, being of one substance with the Father . . ."[18]

Though the theologians almost unanimously agreed with the Nicene Creed, it was mere lip service to many of them. The controversy continued, and Athanasius entered the fray. He constantly wrote against and debated Arianism, and this riled religious and political authorities in the Roman Empire. He was maligned, falsely accused, attacked, and exiled, but he always stood firm. Finally, eight years after his death, at the Council of Constantinople in 381 A.D. the church ratified and expanded the Nicene Creed (and the church gained a consensus concerning the deity of Christ and the Trinity).

You may ask, "So what? What difference does this make in my life?" Well, how do you think Athanasius was able to stand firm, to delight in the Lord, to hold fast to the truth of Christ's deity amidst such degradation, accusation, and exile? One thing mightily helpful to him was the truth of Ephesians 1:12. Most English translations of this verse do not do it justice. Consider my literal translation, keeping in mind the Greek word order, "to the end or purpose of His praise glory, we who were pre-hoping in the Messiah." You must read verses ten through twelve as one thought. Christ Jesus is the household manager, the Chief Operating Officer, the Economist who will sum up again all things in Himself, the One who will make all things right on that great day. More specifically, the lot you have received from the Father, the details of your life, were foreordained by Him who is constantly working in your life to bring about His purpose, a purpose that ultimately is for His own praise and glory. In order for us to live this out, to trust what God is doing, it is vital that we pre-hope in Christ, that we hope with a future expectation of fulfillment. We see this idea constantly taught in Scripture, (see Romans 8:24–25, Romans 15:12, 1 Corinthians 15:19). Like a woman in labor, like a tri-athlete finishing the Iron Man competition, so we endure present pain and suffering looking for the payoff, the time of fulfillment and joy, the final redemption of our bodies.

The only way you can pre-hope in the Messiah, the Lord Jesus our Prophet, Priest, and King, is to know God better, to trust Him in His attributes. Consider three of them. First is His *aseity* (from the Latin *a se*, meaning from Himself). God is self-existent, independent of us, (see Psalm 115:3, Isaiah 45:6–7, Acts 17:24–25). God is not helped or hindered

---

18. Piper, *Contending for Our All: Defending Truth and Treasuring Christ in the Lives of Athanasius, John Owen, and J. Gresham Machen*, 45ff.

by anything we do or do not do. He does as He pleases because He is sovereign. If we stop here, however, then God seems capricious, arbitrary, austere, cold, like the god of the Muslims. Second, our God is also filled with goodness, meaning that all He is and does is worthy of praise, (see Psalm 100:5, Psalm 145:14–16). Everything God does is motivated by His goodness. Ultimately we must say that all He does is good. But we must go further, which brings us to the third attribute. God is also wise, meaning He always does the right thing at the right time, the first time, every time. He makes no mistakes. His timing and execution are impeccable, (see Isaiah 40:13–14, Job 12:13).

What is your lot in life? Suffering is normative. It is not the exception but the rule. Are you willing to pre-hope in Christ by growing in your practical, experiential understanding of His aseity, goodness, and wisdom?

But why does God allow or bring suffering? Why must this be our foreordained lot? Secondarily because He knows that suffering weans us from the world, drives us to Christ for salvation, keeps us as believers at the foot of the cross, and sanctifies us, makes us more holy, (see 1 Peter 5:10). But primarily because He is worthy of our praise and everything He does is calculated to bring praise to Him. This statement would be arrogant if it were not made by God Himself. You see, our Savior is, to use the words of Jonathan Edwards, "All together lovely." Seek after a deeper, greater, more experiential knowledge of the Triune God and His attributes. As you do, you will find that your ability to pre-hope in Christ will grow and flourish.

Knowledge

*. . . that the God of our Lord Jesus Christ, the Father of glory, may give you
a spirit of wisdom and of revelation in the knowledge of Him.*

EPHESIANS 1:17

AARON BURR WAS LESS than two years old when his father, the president of Princeton, died suddenly and unexpectedly in September 1758. A few months later Aaron's Grandfather Jonathan Edwards, who had been elected President of Princeton to succeed his son-in-law, died from complications due to a small pox inoculation. A few months after that Aaron's Grandmother Sarah Edwards died, and finally his mother, Esther Edwards Burr died. Thus in less than one year little Aaron Burr lost both his parents and grandparents.[19] By his teen years during his studies at Princeton, Burr consciously and willfully rejected the faith of his parents and grandparents. In time he became vice president of the United States, serving with President Thomas Jefferson. Most historians consider Burr a political scoundrel, the first in a long, sordid line of machine politicians. When people from his home state of New York wished for him to run for Governor, his long time nemesis, Alexander Hamilton, spoke privately of Burr's dishonesty and unfitness for office. When such information surfaced publicly, Burr felt his character was besmirched, and as was customary in that day, challenged Hamilton to a duel. Hamilton reluctantly agreed but then chose not to fire his gun at his opponent. Burr had no such hesitation and killed Hamilton on the spot. Burr fled first to Maryland, and then to his good friend Colonel Butler on a plantation at what is now St. Simons Island, Georgia. Later Burr was charged with sedition but acquitted. He is buried at the feet of his parents and grandparents

---

19. Murray, *Jonathan Edwards: A New Biography*, 445.

in the cemetery at Princeton, this being one of his last requests, saying that he was unworthy to be buried beside them.[20]

Young Aaron Burr certainly faced very difficult tests of faith, and we may wonder how well we would hold up under similar circumstances. May I suggest, however, that tests of faith, hardship, and trial are normative in the Christian life? The question is—how well will you weather them? Paul, in Ephesians 1:17, after saying he makes mention of the Ephesian believers in his prayers, gives us the purpose for his prayer. He prays that the God of our Lord Jesus Christ, the Father of glory, may give them a Spirit of wisdom (applied knowledge) and of revelation [21](apocalypse, an unveiling or making known) in the knowledge (super-charged, abundant, experiential) of God. Paul knows how vital it is for these believers to grow constantly in the grace and knowledge of Christ. If you live in New England or the Midwest, then you know winter is coming. You must prepare for it. If you live on the Gulf Coast and you hear that a hurricane is coming, then you prepare. Likewise Paul, knowing the normative nature of the tests of faith wants us to prepare for them. This preparation requires an abiding (Psalm 42:5), deepening (Psalm 139:1ff), growing (Psalm 73:28), and living (Habakkuk 3:17ff) knowledge of God. A superficial one (see Psalm 73:10–14) or a stale one (like Demas in Colossians 4:14, 2 Timothy 4:10) simply will not do.

Contrast John Winthrop with Aaron Burr. Winthrop left for the New World in 1630 at the age of forty-two and became the governor of Massachusetts Bay. He came with a little over three hundred people, and within the first six months, two hundred of them had died. His first two wives died from complications in child birth. Of his four daughters, three died in infancy and the fourth died in her twenties. His oldest son Henry drowned shortly after arriving in Boston. His younger son Forth, a promising candidate for the Puritan pastoral ministry, died shortly after John left for the New World. And his steward, due either to ineptness or dishonesty, nearly brought Winthrop to financial ruin. Yet in all these trials, these tests of faith, John and Margaret Winthrop never doubted God. He remained their one, true constant and abiding hope.[22]

---

20. Ibid.

21. Many commentators believe this is the Holy Spirit (see John 15:26, the Spirit of truth, and Romans 8:15, the Spirit of adoption).

22. Morgan, The Puritan Dilemma, 175.

The greater your knowledge of God then the greater will be your peace, if applied in faith. Jesus tells us at the end of the Sermon on the Mount (Matthew 7:24ff) that to listen and obey Him means to build our house on a rock, but not to listen means we build our house on sand. The storms of life are sure to come, and a house built on a weak foundation will be swept away. What are your tests of faith? Are you prepared to face the storms that are sure to come? On what are you building your hopes? To build on sand is to be man-centered, to view life as being fundamentally about your own comforts, desires, happiness, and prosperity. When you build in this way, without putting a growing, experiential knowledge of God as your foundation, then when the storms of life come you will be given to disappointment with God, disillusionment with your place in His plan, and despair over your future. But if you build with a growing, living, abiding, and deepening experiential knowledge of God, then you will begin to see all of life's circumstances as being under His sovereign control. You will see that God's primary aim in everything, including your salvation, sanctification, and glorification is His own glory. For a mere human to make such a claim is audacious and arrogant. Not so, however with the God of creation. He is in heaven and does as He pleases. He has established His throne in the heavens and His sovereignty rules over all.

May God give you a growing, living, deepening, and abiding experiential knowledge of Him! This knowledge is the essence of revival living. How can you get there? You can purpose to become a theologian of the heart by reading a good book or two on systematic theology. A good place to start is the *Westminster Confession of Faith*.[23] But you should always look to Jesus. In Luke 7 we read of Jesus raising from the dead the son of a grieving mother, and such is the power of the Triune God. This power indwells every believer. You are to look in faith for His sustaining and sanctifying grace just as you did for your initial salvation. May God so work in you that the coming storms of life reveal a deep, viable, and true knowledge of Him!

23. Written in 1643 by Puritan theologians in England under the direction of the British Parliament.

Hope, Riches, Power

... the hope of His calling, the riches of the glory of His inheritance in the saints, the surpassing greatness of His power toward us who believe.

EPHESIANS 1:18–19

WE TEND TO FIGHT personal sin in two ways. The first is separatism. Roger Williams came to the Massachusetts Bay Colony in February 1631. He had studied at Cambridge and been tutored there by the great Puritan John Owen. When John Wilson, pastor of the Congregational Church in Boston left to fetch his wife from England, the church asked Williams to be their pastor. Much to their surprise he declined, saying that they were too closely tied to the Church of England, which allowed in its membership drunkards and whores. Williams was then approached by the Congregational Church at Salem, but he declined for the same reason. Then William Bradford and the Plymouth Colony of Pilgrims, separatists in their own right, asked Williams to be their pastor and he again declined saying that he would not fellowship with them. That is because some of their members, when returning to England, worshipped with Anglicans. Later, due to divisiveness, Governor Winthrop and the magistrates of the Massachusetts Bay Colony banished Williams to Narragansett, later called Rhode Island.[24]

The second way we tend to fight personal sin is through emotionalism. Anne Hutchinson and her husband came to the Bay in 1634 to follow John Cotton, the great Puritan preacher who had migrated there from England. Hutchinson was a very capable theologian and bible teacher and held a weekly study for women. First she led a discussion on Cotton's previous Lord's Day sermon, but then she would launch into her peculiar doctrines. One of these beliefs was her view on the sealing of the Holy Spirit. She believed this was subsequent to regeneration, something that

---

24. Gaustad, *Libery of Conscience: Roger Williams in America*, 44ff.

many Puritans of the day taught. However she took this view much farther. She said that when the sealing with the Spirit came, one no longer needed biblical revelation as a guide, one was then able to receive direct revelation from God. Later when she was tried by Winthrop and the magistrates, she said that God told her they would be cursed for prosecuting her, that He would bring destruction on them for the Lord had spoken. She too was banished to Rhode Island.

We overcome sin in this fallen world, not by focusing on it, but by dwelling on our hope, riches, and power in Jesus. Perhaps your tendency is separatism, believing that perfection or near perfection can be reached in this life by withdrawing from the public forum. The Pharisees taught separatism, as did the Pilgrims and modern day fundamentalists. I am not saying that we should allow ourselves or our children to be exposed to any and all evil. Obviously we need to guard our hearts and minds against filth. But I am saying separatism eventually leads to pride, self-righteousness, and lack of love. When the leaders in Massachusetts Bay were approached by the Colony of Virginia for shot and gun powder to repel Indian attacks, the Colony refused, saying that Virginia was not holy enough to warrant their help. We see this today when Christians refuse to help HIV-positive homosexual men, saying that they are not worthy of their aid. You know you are given over to separatism when you think you alone, or your church or denomination alone have a corner on the truth, that all others are wrong, that God cannot be blessing them.

Or perhaps your tendency is emotionalism. The French Prophets of the eighteenth century were given to dreams, visions, and ecstatic speech. Preachers like Jonathan Edwards, George Whitefield, and Gilbert Tennent took them to task. Essentially those embracing emotionalism look to experience prior to or in the place of God's revealed will in His word. Charismatics who deny or downplay the significance of God's word in favor of an emotional encounter with God are looking to their own experience to help them fight sin. You are falling into this error when you find worship stale, when you say the preaching of God's word is not enough for you, when you think you need an extra-biblical experience.

We overcome personal sin by realizing the depth of our riches in Christ. By "the hope of His calling" Paul is referring to the certainty of all God promises because He cannot lie. He has called us effectually. He calls all people to love and obey Him; but only the believer, drawn by the Holy Spirit, obeys and submits to Him. A progression is intended here by Paul.

This hope or certainty of our effectual calling makes itself known "in the riches of the glory of His inheritance in the saints." So much could be said here, but I urge you to study carefully Romans 8, 2 Corinthians 5, and Revelation 21. The reality of a new heaven and a new earth, redemption, election, adoption, and glorification are all ours in Jesus Christ. And this inheritance will come to us *by* the "overpowering greatness of His power toward all who believe in Him." The Holy Spirit who created all things out of nothing, the promised and delivered Holy Spirit on Pentecost, the One who raised Jesus from the dead, is the same Holy Spirit who indwells you.

Dear Christian, you are rich beyond measure. Focus on what you have in Jesus, not the sin that so easily entangles you. If you have ten million dollars and someone wants you to invest in a get-rich-quick scheme, you will not be tempted to go for it. Why? Because you are already rich. You don't need the money. Likewise, when you understand all you have in Jesus, then you do not wish to go after worldly temptations. So put away your fear and your tendency to separate from others. Put away your desire to have something more than what God has prescribed in His word. Dwell on who you are, and on what God has given you. When you do, then separatism and emotionalism will become redundant and superfluous.

Prepare

Behold, I am about to remove you from the face of the earth.
This year you are going to die.

JEREMIAH 28:16

THE NEWLY ELECTED AND installed president of Princeton College, Jonathan Edwards, took over for his son-in-law Aaron Burr Sr. after Burr's death. Edwards died a few months later in March 1758 from complications of a small pox inoculation. Shortly after Edwards' death Samuel Davies, a Presbyterian evangelist from Hanover County, Virginia, became president of Princeton. Davies preached a sermon January 1, 1761 to the students of Princeton from Jeremiah 28:15–17, the account of Hananiah the false prophet whom Jeremiah said would die that very year. Davies was giving a sober warning to the students of Princeton, exhorting them to be prepared to meet their God. Davies himself died unexpectedly a few months after this sermon, preaching as one historian wrote, his own funeral.[25]

As you begin a new year or celebrate your birthday, perhaps you should ask yourself this question—are you prepared to meet your God? There really is no more important question than this one. When one closes his eyes in death and sees for the first time either the glories of heaven or the horrors of hell, nothing in his life, neither his accomplishments nor disappointments will matter. Are you prepared to meet God?

I urge you to prepare yourself on three levels—economically, relationally, and eternally. By economically I have in mind the exhortation of Proverbs 6:6ff, where we are urged to consider the planning of the ant. We are to put away lethargy and laziness and to pursue diligence. Work, tithe, save, procure adequate insurance for your family, invest, and make sure you have a will. By relationally I mean leave nothing unsaid or undone with anyone. Jesus tells us in Matthew 5:23–24 that if we are presenting

---

25. Davies, *Sermons by the Reverend Samuel Davies,* in 3 volumes, volume 2, 195.

our offering before the altar and remember that someone has something against us, then we are to leave our offering, go and be reconciled (the Greek word has the idea of renewing again one's friendship) to our brother, and then come and present our offering. Paul in Ephesians 4:26 gives a series of practical exhortations, among other things saying that we are to let no unwholesome words proceed from our mouths, that we are to be kind to one another, tender hearted, forgiving one another, just as God in Christ has forgiven us. We are to be angry and not sin, not allowing the sun to go down on our anger. Are there any people in your life from whom you are now estranged? You don't want these people leaving this world with things unsaid or undone between you. The guilt you experience will be painful. Are their people in your life with whom this year you ought to resurrect a relationship? My friend Henry Krabbendam of Covenant College has said that love always moves toward the person. Are you doing so?

But by far the most important area in which you are to be prepared to meet God is the eternal one. Surely there are some who are reading this book who will not be on the earth this time next year. It may be you, it may be me. Are you prepared to meet God? Asahel Nettleton, the great nineteenth century Presbyterian evangelist, said that we ought to spend a few moments every day contemplating the glories of heaven and the horrors of hell.[26] Consider, for a moment, the horrors of hell. Jesus defined and made more vivid the doctrine of hell as a place of conscious, endless torment. (See Mark 9:42ff, Matthew 25:41.) Some theologians are now suggesting annihilation, that the soul in hell eventually is destroyed. In this view the unregenerate suffer there for a time, but then God in His mercy destroys the soul so that suffering is not eternal. Every argument I have read proposing annihilation can be reduced to an emotional one. Scripture is plain in what it says. Hell is forever. It is awful beyond our imagination. Is God unfair in condemning people to hell forever? Not at all. Ezekiel 16 is a graphic picture of Judah being rescued, lying in her blood and afterbirth, being taken in by Yahweh, loved, instructed, and provided for. The prophet says that in response to Yahweh's grace Judah has played the harlot, spreading her legs to everyone who passes by. Jonathan Edwards suggested that the higher one's position, the more we are responsible to that person. Thus when we violate that person, the more judgment we deserve. One who poorly treats a sibling who has treated him badly may deserve some punishment; but one who has treated poorly a sibling who has been magnanimous to him deserves a greater punish-

26. Tyler, *The Life and Labours of Asahel Nettleton*, 132.

ment. One who treats a father poorly who has neglected him may deserve some judgment, but one who has hated a loving father surely deserves a greater judgment. How much truer is it to say that man, who has rejected, hated, and mocked God who has so abundantly blessed him with every good thing to enjoy deserves condemnation. How much more does man deserve to be cast into hell forever when he rejects the lover of His soul?[27] Indeed those who die without Christ go to hell where the fire is never quenched and the worm never dies. Are you not yet a Christian? Come to Christ now, humbly repenting, confessing your sin and need of a Savior. He will receive you, forgive you, and take you to heaven when you die.

And if you are a believer, then contemplate the glories of heaven that await you. As glorious as heaven is, it is not the final state. Theologians refer to heaven as the intermediate state. Revelation 19–21 is a vivid picture of heaven, and surely it is wondrous. But there is something even better: the new heaven and new earth (2 Peter 3:13, Isaiah 65:17ff). Dear Christian, when you die your soul immediately enters the glorious presence of Jesus Christ, where you will see Him in all His resurrected glory (Revelation 1:13ff). It is as though you will enter a vast room inhabited by people of every tongue, tribe, and nation, all the saints of all the ages. The focal point will be the risen, glorified Christ. But a day will come when Christ returns to earth, and all will be raised to meet Him. Believers will be given glorified bodies, (1 Corinthians 15:42–44), and will dwell on the new earth with Christ ruling there forever. Practically, this new heaven and earth means the physical pain and suffering you or your redeemed loved ones experienced on earth will be no more. The body will be made perfect. Never again will there be pain, disease, death, hatred, war, or injustice. The glory of God will dwell there. Christ will rule there. And the earth will be restored to its pre-fall condition.

Now in this life you need to cultivate a taste for heaven and the new earth. Perhaps you, even though a Christian are too enamored with this world. It's like taking a teen who loves hip hop music to a symphony. He is bored with it because he has not acquired a taste for better music. Heaven may seem boring to you because you don't think on it enough. You are not preparing yourself enough for it. Think on your loved ones there. See the risen Christ receiving praise from all who reside there. Dwell on the marvelous promise that you will receive a glorified body. Prepare to meet God.

27. Edwards, *The Wrath of Almighty God: Jonathan Edwards on God's Judgment against Sinners*, 87.

Gaining a Biblical Perspective

And you were dead in your trespasses and sin.

EPHESIANS 2:1

ONE DOES NOT LIVE long in Connecticut before hearing the founder of Hartford, the Puritan Thomas Hooker, severely maligned for his handling of the Pequot Indian massacre in 1637. The party line in Connecticut is that Hooker was culpable in the slaughter and annihilation of the Pequot tribe, which lived near Old Saybrook. I have done a fair amount of reading on the issue, and it appears to be a classic "tit for tat" situation. Hooker, with one hundred or so of his church members came to the Massachusetts Bay Colony from England in the early 1630's. He soon petitioned John Winthrop to allow his people to remove themselves from Roxbury, just outside Boston. They desired to settle in the Connecticut River valley, which was far more suitable for farming. Hooker and his people settled Hartford in 1636, and during this time a few men from Boston made a raid on the Pequots near Old Saybrook. Some say the Pequots started it, and others say the Puritans did. We know that the Niantic tribe, living on Block Island, killed a trader named John Oldham, and John Endicott was directed by the General Court in Boston, in August 1636 to retaliate. He did so, raiding Block Island and burning down their dwellings. Later several raids were made by the Pequots on English settlers, first in Old Saybrook but then further inland, reaching Wethersfield, only a few miles from Hartford. They killed nine settlers and kidnapped two young girls. This was unnerving to the settlers, and the General Court in Hartford commissioned John Mason and an army of ninety-nine, including Mohegan and Narragansett Indians as allies (these tribes were having their own problems with the Pequots). They were to take care of the Pequots. Hooker's only involvement in the affair was to preach a sermon stressing their just cause. He also prayed for God to give the army victory over their enemies. The consequent raid on a Pequot fort killed five hundred, including women and children. Only five or six survived the attack. Certainly this act was not a pretty sight, but it was the way warfare was done in the seventeenth century. It is clear that Hooker was not responsible for initiating the battle.[28]

I bring up this event because it appears that Thomas Hooker was falsely accused. Have you ever been falsely accused? Let's be honest, for most of us the false accusations we have experienced always bear some resemblance to the facts. In other words, most of us are culpable in some way. But even if we are not, how should we handle these things?

Paul makes a practical application to the Ephesian Christians in Ephesians 2:1ff, building on what he has written earlier, proclaiming the wondrous truth of God's electing grace, Christ's redeeming blood, and the Spirit's sealing power. He has prayed for them, asking God to work three things mightily in them so that they may experience the fullness of life in Christ. Now he says that prior to their conversion, they were dead in their trespasses and sins. By dead Paul does not mean ill, or near death. He does not mean physical death. He means spiritual death, that their souls had been separated from the life of God, like an astronaut in a space cut off from his life line, like a scuba diver who loses his oxygen tank while fifty feet under the water's surface. This separation means they had no ability or desire to come to God. They had no interest or understanding of the things of God. They were dead in their trespasses and sins. Trespass means to fall, to wander off the path. It is passive in nature, like floating on a raft at the beach, falling asleep, waking up thirty minutes later, realizing you are half a mile down the beach. A trespass is when you purpose to love your wife better, to be more considerate, more involved in the leadership of your children, but then simply drift from it. A trespass is when you purpose to support your husband better, to be more submissive, but then find yourself falling into old patterns when the stresses of life increase. These stresses cause you to go back to your sinful pattern. Sin is more active. The word means to miss the mark. The Ten Commandments tell you exactly what you are to do but you sin when you willfully choose to go your own way. A man who lies, who goes after another woman, or who looks at porn is someone who misses the mark. He knows exactly what he is doing and he does it because he wants to do it.

28. Collingwood, *Thomas Hooker, 1586–1647: Father of Democracy,* 127.

"But God" are two of the greatest words in Holy Scripture. Paul says in Ephesians 2:4. "But God, being rich in mercy, because of His great love with which He loved us . . ." Understand this dear Christian, and burn this deeply into your mind and heart—prior to your conversion you had absolutely no ability or desire to come to Christ. You were completely lost, outside of Christ, on the road to hell. You did not choose God. He chose you, and He did so from sheer mercy for His own glory. He made you spiritually alive. Get out of your mind once and for all the God-demeaning, self-exalting notion that you had something to do with your salvation. You were dead. Can a dead man understand anything? Can he do anything?

There are so many practical applications we can make to this glorious truth—"You were dead in your trespasses and sins, but God . . . ." But here's one to chew on for a while. If you have the forgiveness of your sins, if you once were dead but now are alive in Christ Jesus, if you are united to Him, if you are indwelt by the Holy Spirit, then can we not say that you have everything you need? When the four men brought the paralytic to Jesus (Mark 2:1ff) the first thing Jesus said to the man was, "My son, your sins are forgiven." What? Was Jesus being cruel and insensitive to the man? Was He merely giving him spiritual platitudes like we so often do when someone comes to us, pouring out their hearts, and we say, "Brother, I am sorry. I will pray for you." Not at all! Jesus knew that the man's greatest need was to be right with God, to know that his sins were forgiven.

Here's the truth. You think you need a wife. You think you need a better wife. You think you need a husband, or a better, more loving husband. You think you need more money, a better job, better children. You think you need better health, more or better friends. You feel sorry for yourself because you have been falsely accused. The truth is this, dear Christian— you really have all you need. No matter what happens to you, no matter how difficult things may become for you, no matter how long these things may stay with you; your sins are forgiven. You are loved by the Father. You are redeemed by the blood of Christ. You have the indwelling Holy Spirit. You are going to heaven when you die. You have a friend who sticks closer than a brother. You have a Savior who is preparing a mansion for you in heaven. So get a Biblical perspective on your situation. Quit complaining and whining about how hard you have it. You have Christ, and He is all you need.

The Purpose of Suffering

I would have despaired unless I had believed
that I would see the goodness of the Lord in the land of the living.

PSALM 27:13

JOHN CALVIN'S BIOGRAPHER EMANUEL Stickelberger gives a litany of ailments the great Reformer suffered during his life.

> . . . He was afflicted with a headache concentrated on one side which hardly ever left him during his life . . . during many a night he was 'inhumanly' tormented by them. Subjected to maladies of the trachea, he had with pains in his side to spit blood when he had used his voice too much in the pulpit. Several attacks of pleurisy prepared the way for consumption (tuberculosis of the lungs) whose helpless victim he became at the age of fifty-one. Constantly he suffered from the hemorrhoidal vein, the pains of which were unbearably increased by an internal abscess that would not heal. Several times intermittent fever laid him low, sapping his strength and constantly reducing it. He was plagued by gallstones and kidney stones in addition to stomach cramps and wicked intestinal influenzas. To all this there was finally added arthritis.

Calvin's suffering did not end with himself however. His wife died after only nine years of marriage, and he suffered the early deaths of all three of his children.[29]

God allows, brings, and even foreordains our suffering. Isaiah says that the Lord is God and that there is no other, the One forming light and creating darkness, causing well being and creating calamity, (see Isaiah 45:6–7). The question is why? Why did John Calvin suffer so much? Was God paying him back for some secret sin? If God loved John Calvin, then why would He allow, bring, or even foreordain this unimaginable suffer-

---

29. Stickelberger, *Calvin*, translated by David George Gelzer, 86, 87.

41

ing? Why does God allow, bring, and foreordain the suffering through which you have walked in your life?

There are three reasons for the suffering of all the saints in Christ Jesus. We suffer for the manifestation of God's glory, the sanctification of His church, and the salvation of His elect. Let's take these one at a time. First is the manifestation of God's glory. Psalm 115:3 makes clear that God is in His heaven, and He does as He pleases. In Isaiah 46:10ff God speaks and says, "My purpose will be established, and I will accomplish all My good pleasure . . . Truly I have spoken; truly I will bring it to pass. I have planned it, surely I will do it." Isaiah gives thanks to God for all His wondrous works, plans formed long ago with perfect faithfulness, (Isaiah 25:1). Psalm 67 says, "God be gracious to us, and cause His face to shine upon us, that Thy way may be known on the earth, Thy salvation among all nations." Because He is God, the eternal, transcendent, holy, sovereign, and righteous God, He alone is worthy of praise; and because He is Creator He can do with His creation what He desires for His own glory and praise. Everything that happens in the world, even the evil that God allows, ultimately is to bring glory to His name.

And when God brings suffering to His people, it always is to wean us from the world. Just as a nursing mother, at some point, weans her infant from breast milk, causing the child to become increasingly less dependent upon her; so God uses suffering to wean us from our delight and trust in the things of this world. That's why the Psalmist, who had suffered terribly as he saw the prosperity of the wicked, eventually was able to say, "Whom have I in heaven, but Thee. And besides Thee, I desire nothing on earth," (Psalm 73:25). Do you see God in your suffering? Are you able to trust Him, knowing that this is for His glory? Do you see that this suffering is to wean you from your dependence on creation? Can you see that it is to be a catalyst for comfort and satisfaction?

Second, God allows, brings, and foreordains suffering for the sanctification of His church. Paul makes a profound statement in Colossians 1:24 about his own suffering, "Now I rejoice in my suffering for your sake, and in my flesh I do my share on behalf of His body (which is the church) in filling up that which is lacking in Christ's afflictions." Paul cannot mean that his suffering or any believer's suffering, for that matter, adds to the merits of Christ's suffering to bring us eternal salvation. Only Christ's suffering, death, and resurrection make possible our right standing before God. What does Paul mean then? He means that the suffering through which he has gone in the work of the gospel adds to and helps complete the body of Christ, His church. Christ is the head of His church and His suffering was redemptive or salvific. But we are members of His body, perhaps no more than a toe or a strand of hair, but all of us in His body suffer in some way. This enables us to identify with other believers, giving us a tangible expression of unity with them all over the world and throughout history. Paul has the same idea in mind in 1 Corinthians 12:26, "And if one member suffers, all the members suffer with it, if one member is honored, all the members rejoice with it." And God uses these sufferings to drive us to Jesus, the only place of refuge. In Psalm 2:12, David says, "Do homage to the Son, lest He become angry, and you perish in the way, for His wrath may soon be kindled. How blessed are all who take refuge in Him!" God uses the suffering through which you have gone to drive you to Christ, to show you there is no other fountain from which you can drink for comfort, solace, grace.

Finally God allows, brings, and foreordains suffering for the salvation of His elect. In 2 Thessalonians 1:4ff Paul is complementing the Thessalonians on their perseverance and faith in the midst of persecutions and afflictions. He says that their suffering is an indication of God's righteous judgment so that they may be considered worthy of the kingdom of God for which they had been suffering. He goes on to say that God will deal out retribution to all who disobey the gospel, promising that the Lord Jesus will be revealed from heaven with His mighty angels in flaming fire when He comes to be glorified in His saints. The only way to explain the genocide, the persecution, and the untold suffering of God's people throughout the ages is to know that God's ultimate purpose for everything is the salvation of His people to the praise of His own glory. Nothing else makes sense. And when God's people are in the midst of suffering it drives them to long for heaven, to say with heartfelt earnestness, "I would have despaired if I had not believed I would see the goodness of the Lord in the land of the living."

Calvin knew this truth and it is what sustained him all his days. Will you see God? Will you trust God? Will you wait on God? He has you right where He wants you. Your suffering is not an accident. It is not bad luck. It is not fate. It is not "payback time." It is for the manifestation of God's glory, the sanctification of His church, and the salvation of His people.

But God

*But God, being rich in mercy, because of His great love
with which He loved us.*

Ephesians 2:4

H E WAS BORN IN 1712 and reared a Calvinist in Geneva. He came
from a well-to-do family, and his mother died when he was an infant. He had one sibling, a brother seven years his senior. His father loved
his brother but despised him. He gave us cold baths, weekend cottages,
and the notion that sports build character. He also gave us sordid, un-
toward things like totalitarianism and the state as our father, the one who
provides our education and care for the poor. He had several mistresses,
one of whom bore him five children. Due to the exalted view he had of
himself, thinking he was far too important to be relegated to things like
caring for children, he abandoned them all. He left them to die. He was
credited as the major catalyst for the French Revolution, and though he
died ten years before it began his ashes were spread in the Pantheon in
Paris out of respect for him. I am referring to Jean-Jacques Rousseau.[30]

He left the faith of his fathers, and entered into a godless way of life
that has destroyed millions in the last two hundred and thirty years. While
none of you reading this have succumbed to the unbelief of Rousseau, you
nonetheless are prone to wander from the faith. We are prone to doubt
and unbelief. Why? For at least two reasons. First, we are affected by the
post modern concept of reality. We are told that a god resides within each
of us, and that our primary task is to get to know this god. We are to think
good thoughts of him. We are to get in touch with the deity within. But
nothing of life changing power comes from within ourselves. Our most
profound thinkers, even our best philosophers can only diagnose problems. They cannot bring necessary change. Second, we tend tragically to

30. Johnson, *Intellectuals*, 4.

44

begin in the wrong place. We tend to begin with ourselves or our circumstances. Consequently our view of God is far too small. He is an anemic, effeminate, weak, local, tribal, Johnny-come-lately deity. He cannot help when the chips are down, when we find ourselves in despair.

This Johnny-come-lately deity is not the God of the Apostle Paul. Instead, Paul speaks of a strong, transcendent, all powerful God who is mighty to save and deliver. The construction of the first seven verses of Ephesians 2 is quite emphatic. Paul begins by putting the object at the beginning of the sentence, verses 1 to 3. Next he places the subject, "But God", at the beginning of verse 4. He then adds the predicate, "made us alive together", after that. Paul goes on to stress three vital words—mercy, love, and grace. Mercy has the idea of pity and compassion, of seeing someone in need and having the ability and desire to relieve the suffering. Jesus raising Lazarus from the dead is a good example of mercy. He was deeply moved within by the suffering of Mary and Martha. The love Paul mentions is the feeling and consequent action of God toward sinners. Jesus prays to His Father in John 17:26, "and I have made Thy name known to them, and will make it known; that the love wherewith Thou didst love Me may be in them, and I in them." The Apostle John says, "And this is love. Not that we loved God but that He loved us and gave His Son as an atoning sacrifice for our sins," 1 John 4:10. And the word grace means pardon for the guilty, the one justly condemned. Gerald Ford's pardon of Richard Nixon after he resigned the presidency in 1974 comes to mind as an example of grace.

What makes God's mercy, love, and grace even more remarkable is what Paul lays down about us in verses 1–3. He says that we were dead in our sins, that we walked according to the spirit of the age, that we were under the control of the devil, that we creatively indulged the desires of our flesh and mind. Thus we deserved judgment in hell.

Dear Christian the two greatest words in all of Scripture are "But God." The waters had covered the highest mountains, killing all cattle and beasts, but God preserved Noah in the ark along with all the animals with him. David was on the run from Saul, living in the mountains and wilderness as Saul sought daily to kill him, but God did not allow David to fall into his hands. While we were still helpless Christ died for the ungodly. Though some may dare to die for a righteous man God demonstrates His own love for us in that while we were yet sinners, Christ died for us. Jesus was delivered up by the predetermined plan and foreknowledge of God to godless men who put Him to death by nailing Him to the cross; but God raised Him from the dead, putting an end to the agony of death.

Can you not therefore be on the alert, stand firm in the faith, act like men, and be strong? Can you not do all things without grumbling or disputing? Can you not obey Jesus who said, "Do not worry about anything. Is not life more than food, and the body than clothing?" Can you not trust God to save your loved one? Can you not trust God to sustain you in a terrible marriage? You may say, "You have no idea how hard-hearted and wicked my brother is." But God . . . You may say, "My marriage is hopelessly broken. I have tried everything." But God.

Jesus told the man with the possessed son (Mark 9:14ff), "All things are possible to him who believes." This statement cannot mean that God will do anything we ask, if we only have enough faith. Paul prayed three times for the removal of the thorn in his flesh, and God said, "No." Jesus prayed for the cup to pass from Him in the Garden of Gethsemane and the Father said, "No." What Jesus means here is this—if you have faith in the great God of scripture, the One described as the author of salvation, creation, and providence; then He will give you the grace to do what you ought to do. He will give you the grace to do His will, and His will is found in His word. Believe what God says and act upon it.

Listen to God

But God ... even when we were dead in our transgressions, made us alive together with Christ (by grace you have been saved).

EPHESIANS 2:5

OH THE FOLLY OF exchanging the truth of God for a lie! Oh the folly of creating a substitute for the truth of God. Israel did it after God had manifested His glory in their deliverance from Egyptian bondage, performing the ten plagues, parting the Red Sea for them to walk through, bringing the waters down upon the Egyptian army, and killing all of them. Shortly after this, however, Moses went to the mountain to meet God, and to receive the Ten Commandments. While there Israel made a golden calf, creating a substitute for the real thing.

You do the same thing. You tend to live with the guilt and shame of your past sins, constantly replaying them in your mind. To be sure, you ought to grieve over your past sin. You may experience consequences from your past sin, and you certainly ought to right any wrongs you can from your past sins. However you never again are to feel shame or guilt from them. When you do, then you can expect despair, anxiety, and fear. You also tend to live with the guilt and shame of past sins done to you by someone else. You fail to forgive them their wrong to you, holding them hostage to their actions. If you persist, then you will live in bitterness, anger, and resentment. Additionally you are sometimes paralyzed by your present sins, alternating between hiding them and glorying in them. It is one thing to ask a brother or sister to pray for you about your sin, but it is quite another to confess in order to relieve your guilty conscience while secretly hoping your confessor will condone your sin. You are often defeated by your recurring sins, conversely giving in to them and making deals with them. Perhaps you say, "Okay, I know I look at porn and have a wandering eye, but I do tithe and teach Sunday School. I provide for my family. Isn't this behavior good enough?" To be sure, God is gracious and

47

merciful, filled with loving kindness and compassion. He is patient with us in our sin, but His patience is not the same thing as condoning our hypocrisy and our unwillingness to deal with it biblically. Furthermore we sometimes listen to the world's view of sin. What does it say? It tells us to downplay our sin, not to worry about it. It convinces us that a little sin is not a big deal. It also tells us to ignore our sin, to call it a mistake, an accident, a poor choice, a psychological weakness. Our world tells us to project our sin to other people. "I cannot help what I do. My father left me when I was ten years old . . . I was abused as a child . . . I grew up in a dysfunctional family . . . If you had to live with this woman, then you would drink too . . ."

So you listen to yourself. You listen to the world. And you listen to the devil. The accuser of the brethren reminds you of what a loser you are, of how hypocritical you are, of how far short you fall of all the other believers in your church. He loves to remind you that if the preacher really knew what goes on in your house behind closed doors, then he would not welcome you to church.

I ask you this question—*what has listening to yourself, the world, and the devil done for you?* Don't you think it is about time to listen to God? And what does He say? He says that anyone in Christ is a new creation. The old has passed away and the new has come. Or to put it another way, everything about you of importance has changed, if you are in Christ. This claim is not speculation. This statement is not my opinion. This word is not mere Christian tradition. This declaration is fact. In Ephesians 2:5 Paul declares that you are made alive together with Christ. You were dead in your sins. However by the regenerating work of the Holy Spirit, by the marvelous grace of God, you are now alive. This statement means that you have a new heart that loves God and hates sin. Therefore you have a new mind and a new ability to obey God. This truth means that you have new values: you love God's word and His people, and you love world missions and the salvation of sinners. You are united to Christ in His death, burial, and resurrection. This declaration is not merely a legal, federal, objective, or positional truth. It is all these, but many Biblical commentators and preachers stop short of the full meaning of Paul's words. The very context of Ephesians 2:1ff screams out the reality of the experiential. This union with Christ is not merely a nice theological proposition. It is true in the very depths of your soul. You are mystically united to Christ, (John 15:1–5).

Think of it this way. Perhaps you were born with a propensity toward art, music, writing poetry or prose, or engineering. The fact that you have a propensity to do one or more of these things will work itself out in your thoughts and actions. You can improve upon these natural gifts given you by God. In a much greater way you now have a new bent, a new propensity, and a new predisposition toward God, to love Him, worship Him, and obey Him. You must now choose what you will do with these gifts.

In Mark 1:21ff we find that Jesus entered the synagogue at Capernaum on the Sabbath and preached to the crowd. The people were amazed at His teaching for He was teaching as one having authority, and not as the scribes. My friend Geoff Thomas[31] has written that the word *amazed* here means these folks were at their panic stations, describing how people on an ocean liner feel when it begins to sink. In the same worship service, a demon-possessed man cries out, "What do we have to do with You, Jesus of Nazareth? Have you come to destroy us? I know who You are—the Holy One of God!" Jesus responded to the demon by telling it to shut up and come out of the man. The demon obeyed, and the people once again were amazed, startled, brought to great fear through seeing the authority of Jesus.

Jesus is the same today as He was then, as He always has been. He has the authority to redeem, to cast out demons, to make you a new creation, to kill the old man in you, to set you free from your sin. Why don't you listen to Him? Revival living is couched in obedience and faith.

Have you not listened to yourself long enough? Have you not listened to the lies of the world and of the devil long enough? Put away your folly. Listen to God. Everything of importance has changed about you, if you are in Christ. You are a new creation. You have died with Christ. You have been raised with Christ. Your old man is dead. Your body of sin is being rendered powerless. You are no longer under condemnation. Nothing will separate you from the love of God, which is in Christ Jesus our Lord. Oh the folly of exchanging the truth of God for a lie! Listen to God!

31. Geoff Thomas is the Pastor of the Alfred Place Baptist Church, Aberystwyth, Wales, from his sermon on Mark 1:21ff.

The Love of God

And to know the love of Christ which surpasses knowledge, that you may be filled up to all the fullness of God.

EPHESIANS 3:19

THE DAY AFTER OUR oldest son's wedding in May 2002, my wife was having her private devotional time, praying on her knees, when she was overwhelmed with a sense of God's love for her. The experience was so profound, so unusual, that she has never forgotten it. For at least a year leading up to this time she had a sense of dread, that God would require something difficult of her that she would not or could not do. This fear constricted her life, causing her to be blind to God's goodness, wisdom, and love. But on that day she was deeply reassured of God's love, saying to the Lord, "Whatever it is that you will require of me, I willingly submit to it." Less than a year later, we left the people and church we loved at St. Simons Island, Georgia and ventured to New England to plant a new church.

Martyn Lloyd-Jones the great Welsh preacher said that our problems can be traced back to our doubt or denial of the greatness of the gospel.[32] When you doubt God's love you will be paralyzed with fear—fear that God will bring hardship on you, fear that God will take your children, your spouse, your grandchildren. You will fear rejection from those you love. You will fear the future. You succumb to fear when you look to people, places, and things to comfort you, but these substitutes will eventually disappoint you. They cannot deliver as advertised. Furthermore, to deny or doubt God's love is also to reject the truth of His goodness and wisdom. This denial or doubt will rob you of your joy and freedom. Does God take the people whom we love? Does He bring hardship upon us? Yes, of course. We have all experienced these things; but a profound, deep,

---

32. Lloyd-Jones, *Spiritual Depression: Its Causes and Cure*, 54.

abiding sense of God's love will always draw you back to the truth of what the old Puritan Thomas Watson said, "All God's blows are love."[33]

Paul the Apostle, in the text mentioned above is closing out his marvelous prayer for the Ephesians, what the commentator William Hendriksen[34] calls the top rung of the ladder in his prayer. He is building on what he has already prayed. In addition to being fortified with power by the Holy Spirit in the inner person, in addition to Christ taking up His residence in our hearts by faith, and in addition to being rooted and grounded in love, knowing the breadth, length, height, and depth of Christ's love; Paul also prays that this love of Christ would go way beyond a mere theological knowledge. He desires for this to consume the very essence of every believer. The purpose of such a prayer is that we will be filled up to all the fullness of God. If Jesus is the fullness of deity in bodily form (Colossians 2:9), then being filled up to all the fullness of God means possessing the communicable attributes of God in increasing measure. By this statement he means love, mercy, grace, patience, loving kindness, holiness. In other words, Paul is praying that we may know the over-the-top, other-world, transcendent love of God.

Is it possible, dear believer, that you are missing all God has for you? You have been chosen by the Father, predestinated to His love, adopted into His family, redeemed by the blood of Jesus, sealed with the Spirit until the day of redemption, and made heirs of God and fellow heirs with Christ. You are no longer under condemnation, and nothing will ever separate you from the love of God that is in Christ Jesus our Lord. Yet you still worry. You fear rejection from loved ones. You fear that if you give yourself unreservedly to God, He will zap you with untold hardship. You have some vague fear of the future. Consequently you exhibit little of the fruit of the Spirit—love, joy, peace, patience, kindness, goodness, gentleness, faithfulness, self-control. You have trouble loving different, difficult, and diffident people. Paul says the kingdom of God is not eating or drinking but righteousness, peace, and joy in the Holy Spirit, but you tend to exhibit little of these.

What are you to do? In John 7 the Feast of the Tabernacles is being observed, but Jesus purposely lags behind, not going to Jerusalem with His disciples to observe it. This feast was an annual event, reminding Israel of

33. Watson, *All Things for Good*, 57.

34. Hendriksen, *New Testament Commentary: Exposition of Galatians, Ephesians, Philippians, Colossians, and Philemon*, 173.

God's faithfulness to them in the wilderness, rejoicing over His provision in the harvest of crops, celebrating Yahweh's presence in the pillar of fire by night and the cloud by day, reminding them of the water given them when Moses struck the rock in the wilderness. When Jesus finally comes on the scene, on the last day of the week-long feast, He cried out, "If anyone is thirsty, let him come to Me and drink. He who believes in Me, as the Scripture said, 'From his innermost being will flow rivers of living water.'" This declaration by Jesus was an astounding one, and the Jews immediately knew that He was claiming to be the water provided them in the wilderness. Many of them would remember the words of Isaiah, who prophesied the coming Holy Spirit, symbolized by water, (see Isaiah 44:3, 51:1, 58:11). His disciples would have remembered Jesus' interchange with the Samaritan woman a short time before (John 4:10) where He claimed to be living water.

I doubt that you have ever really been thirsty. I am not talking about going without water during a heavy workout and having dry mouth. No, I am speaking of going without water for two or three days, or being stranded on a mountain trail with a broken leg, unable to move toward water. Those who are truly thirsty are desperate for water. They can think of little else. They know they must have water or they die. They would pay any price for it at such a time. Here's the point—the reason we doubt God's love is because we don't know the fullness of the living water, the Holy Spirit. We don't know this fullness because we are not desperate. I think those in our church who gather every Sunday night to pray for revival, the lost, world missions, and church planting are sensing our own desperation. When I listen to our radio program on the way to church every Sunday morning on a secular talk radio station, I cannot help but wonder, "What are these people thinking?" They are not buying the message. It is too radical, too humbling to hear that they are sinners and need a Savior. But this reality drives me to desperation. I must have the Spirit's presence and power or I can do nothing. If you are desperate for the Holy Spirit, really desperate, really thirsty, then Jesus will fill you. When He does, you then will know in a profound, deep, and abiding way the love of God.

Proof of Power

*Then He said, "Throw it on the ground." So he threw his staff on the
ground, and it became a serpent; and Moses fled from it.*

EXODUS 4:3

N O ONE COULD BLAME John Knox if he doubted God's call on his life.
He saw his friends Patrick Hamilton[35] and George Wishart[36] burned
at the stake for preaching Reformation doctrine. Knox was a galley slave
on a French ship for nineteen months, and then faced threats from
Mary Stuart, Queen of Scotland, after his release and return to Scotland.
Nonetheless Knox was a fearless preacher of grace, one whom God used
powerfully to transform sixteenth century Scotland. Moses too, had
doubts about his call. In Exodus 3 he fears his call and pleads ignorance.
In Exodus 4 he falls into unbelief, unwilling to believe that Yahweh is with
him, calling him and empowering him to be the deliverer of Israel.

What are your doubts? Granted, your calling is nowhere near as
monumental as that of John Knox or Moses. God however still calls you
to be a faithful husband, father, wife, mother, student, business person.
Perhaps your calling seems far too much for you, that you are in over your
head, that perhaps even others are beginning to doubt your position or
status with your company. What are you to do?

One of the more remarkable and recurring themes in Scripture is
God's condescension, how He stoops to our weakness, meeting us right
where we are. In the midst of Moses' unbelief Yahweh performs three
successive signs, all meant to prove to Moses, Israel, and Pharaoh that
indeed He has called Moses to be Israel's great deliverer. In Exodus 4:1–5
Yahweh turns the staff (a symbol of Egyptian power and authority over
surrounding nations) into a serpent. Magicians in Egypt, using sleight of

---

35. Knox, *The Reformation in Scotland*, 5.
36. Ibid., 63.

53

hand, gave the impression of turning staffs into serpents. Yahweh does the real thing. This sign symbolizes Yahweh's sovereignty over the nations. In verses 6–7 Yahweh tells Moses to put his hand in his bosom, and it is transformed into leprous skin (the Hebrew word is often used to denote various skin diseases). Skin diseases were signs of covenantal curses,[37] (see Deuteronomy 28:27). Upon Yahweh's command Moses put his hand back into his bosom, and it was restored to its original condition. This symbolizes Yahweh's sovereignty in restoration. Yahweh has the power to restore Israel back to Himself, removing the curses and bringing the blessings of the covenant. And in verses 8–9 Yahweh turns the Nile into blood. The Egyptians believed life was in the Nile River. After all Egypt was a desert with little life, just a few miles beyond either bank of the Nile. Yahweh proves by turning the Nile into blood that He is sovereign over creation.

This story is instructive and should build hope in the heart of every discouraged and fearful believer. Moses is guilty of playing the "what if" and "they may say" games. Are you? "What if I am a bad mother? What if I lose my job? How will I pay the mortgage? What if my marriage fails? Then what? What if my child dies? How would I bear it?" To live with fear and doubt paralyzes. Do you play the "they may say" game? Maybe you think, "If I become a parent and my child rebels against me, they may say that I am a terrible parent . . . If I venture out and start a new business and fail, then they may say that I am a good salesman but poor manager . . . If I get married, though I am divorced once already, then others may say that I failed and that I am sure to fail again." You get the picture. Do you play the "what if" and "they may say" game?

How can I help you? May I suggest you overcome your doubts the same way Yahweh is encouraging Moses to do. *Trust what Yahweh has said and done.* Theologians often speak of the three mighty acts of God—creation, providence, and redemption.[38] Each of these parallel the three signs in Exodus 4:1–9. God spoke and all came into being, (Genesis 1:1–2, Job 26:13). That's the mighty work of creation. When Yahweh overruled the natural properties of water, turning it into blood, then this flowed from His creative power. Your doubts about overcoming chronic problems like unbelieving family members, debt, or illness are overcome by realizing that the

37. Currid, *A Study Commentary on Exodus*, 102.
38. Reymond, *A New Systematic Theology of the Christian Faith*, 383.

same power present in creation, the Holy Spirit, also indwells every believer. You have power to conquer or withstand every trial and temptation.

Yahweh transforms the staff into a serpent and back again into a staff. This transformation is a mighty act of providence. Psalm 91 is replete with references to Yahweh's omnipotent care. He says that because we have loved Him, He will deliver us; that He will set us securely on high. He will answer us when we call upon Him, being with us in trouble, rescuing us and honoring us, with a long life satisfying us, enabling us to behold His glorious salvation. When you doubt your role in marriage, rearing children, doing your work, when you fear the death of a child, learn to hold onto the truth about Yahweh's mighty acts of providence. Nothing escapes His notice. Talk to yourself, reminding yourself of these great truths.

And Yahweh transforms Moses' clear skin into leprous skin and back again to clear skin. His is a ministry of restoration, taking away curses and replacing them with blessings. You may look at your speech, actions, attitudes, and your secret sins about which no one else but God knows, and feel hopeless. You may doubt God's love and forgiveness. You may doubt that heaven is your eternal possession. But Jesus has wrought a mighty work of redemption through His blood, the forgiveness of our trespasses according to the riches of His grace, (Ephesians 1:17, Colossians 1:13–14). Consider the miracle in Mark 1:40ff where Jesus heals a leper who makes his way through the crowd, falling down before Him, beseeching Him for help. Jesus, contrary to what the religious leaders of His day did, touched the man, healing him. You, dear Christian, were under the covenantal curses. You were helpless, ungodly, having no hope and without God in this world. But God was rich in mercy toward you, making you alive together with Christ, taking away your sins as far as the east from the west. Stop playing the "what if" and "they may say" game. Hold onto the mighty works of God in creation, providence, and redemption. Remind yourself of all that has happened to you. Forget none of His benefits to you.

Christ's Eternal Session

These are in accordance with the working of the strength of His might
which He brought about in Christ when He raised Him from the dead,
and seated Him at His right hand in the heavenly places.

EPHESIANS 1:19B, 20

WILLIAM CAREY, THE FATHER of modern missions was born in 1761 in Northampton, England, and was a shoemaker from age fourteen to twenty-eight. He became a Christian at age eighteen and married Dollie Plackett when nineteen. She was six years older than he. They could not have been more different.[39] Carey taught himself Latin by the time he was twelve, and mastered Greek, Hebrew, and Dutch a few years later. Dollie on the other hand, was illiterate. She signed her name with an X. When Carey was twenty-eight he sensed a call to become a missionary, and his burden for the heathen of India grew to the point that he offered himself to the Lord for missionary service a few years later. Dollie was very reluctant to leave home, fearing for the safety and health of her three young boys. Finally she relented and the whole family made their way to India. Within months of their arrival their six year old son Peter died of dysentery. This sent Dollie over the edge. She spent long periods of time locked up in her home or an insane asylum, and her boys basically reared themselves. After all, their father was so busy with his missionary work that he neglected them, and when he was home he was too mild-mannered to discipline them. One of the boys, Jabez, became rebellious and lived in debauchery. He finally came to faith in Christ after bringing great heartache to his father for many years.

Does this story bother you? Doesn't this same incongruous? How can God use such a man as William Carey so powerfully when he had serious issues at home? One may ask if he should have gone to the mission

---

39. Rusten, *The One Year Book of Christian History*, 352.

field in the first place, yet it is clear that God mightily blessed his ministry. Let's face it—life can be very messy, very confusing. You have a desire to follow Christ and to pursue holiness, but you have obstacles that slow you down, impede your progress. There are times you even wonder if you are a Christian, especially when you know the sin that lurks secretly in your flesh and mind, things that are so perverse that you would be terribly ashamed if they were revealed to others.

Well take courage dear Christian from Paul's words in these two verses. He is telling us that God overcomes all obstacles in our pursuit of Him, working powerfully in Christ's resurrection and eternal session. Paul is saying that the proof, the demonstration of His work to overcome all obstacles by the hope of our calling, the riches of the glory of our inheritance in the saints, and the surpassing greatness of His power toward us believers is Christ's resurrection and session at the Father's right hand. The Lord Jesus Christ entered into a state of exaltation after His death on the cross—His resurrection, ascension, eternal session, and second coming in judgment. The eternal session of Jesus at the right hand of God is a vital truth in Scripture (see Psalm 110:1, Hebrews 1:3, Hebrews 12:1–2, 1 Corinthians 15:25–26, 1 Peter 3:21–22). His eternal session means many things. I mention only three here. One, it means you are going where Christ now is, (2 Corinthians 5:8). Two, you share in Christ's dominion over all things. You are seated with Him in the heavenly places (Ephesians 1:3, 2:6), and all things are in subjection to Him, (Colossians 1:16–17, Ephesians 1:22). And three, Christ Jesus is destroying all satanic strongholds. He has bound the devil, and He is plundering his house (Matthew 12:28–29, 1 John 3:8, 2 Corinthians 10:4–5, Revelation 20:2), bringing the nations of the world to Himself.

These truths are profound and marvelous, but you still face many obstacles to your pursuit of God. What are they? You battle the lust of the flesh, the lust of the eyes, and the boastful pride of life (2 John 2:16). The lust of the flesh is your craving for comfort which often reveals itself in laziness, lethargy, procrastination, and bad habits. Sometimes you just do not want o eat, rest, or exercise properly. Sometimes you are too lazy to read your bible and pray, to do nothing more than go through the motions at work, to not lead your family as you ought. Then you face the lust of the eyes. This lust is sensuality. Obviously I have in mind sexual sin in the lustful look or pornography, but I also mean more than these things. The lust for things is constantly exposed to our prurient interests by magazine and television ads—the desire for more and more stuff. Then there is the pride of life. This desire is the lust for position that manifests itself in craving notoriety through our work or our children. Then how about the physical, emotional, mental, or psychological problems that often plague us. Paul speaks of the decay of the outer body, (2 Corinthians 4:16–18). This decay saps our spiritual energy, our resolve, much like an amoeba that a star athlete acquires in a third world country. It robs him of his physical endurance and stamina. Sin wears you down, breaks down your resolve and faith. And when this breakdown happens, then the glorious truth of our hope, riches, and power in Jesus begin to wane. They do not have the fervor, appeal, or power to keep us on the highway of holiness.

What are your obstacles, and what are you to do about them? I am not asking you to grit your teeth and simply try to do better. I am asking you to consider, to meditate upon, to feast on this glorious truth—God can and will overcome your every obstacle. Perhaps this victory will not come in this life. You may have to wait until heaven to see it, but the proof that it will come is found in the resurrection and eternal session of the Lord Jesus Christ. So talk to yourself. And what should you say? Try this, "God, you know my weakness and frailty mentally, physically, emotionally. You know my propensity to sin. I grieve over my spiritual declension and I repent, but I need your grace to persevere. I know I can because I am absolutely certain Jesus was raised from the dead. I am certain that He now sits at your right hand. Thus I can and will live in peace because I have dominion with Jesus over all things. I am united to the One who is breaking down all satanic strongholds. And I can live in the future with hope because I know I am going where Jesus now is."

All Jesus Has, You Have

. . . and gave Him as head over all things to the church, which is His body, the fullness of Him who fills all in all.

Ephesians 1:22–23

COTTON MATHER WAS BORN in Boston in 1643, and he came from an illustrious family of preachers. He was named for his two grandfathers, John Cotton and Richard Mather, who were great Puritan preachers in America and England.[40] His father, with whom he co-pastored the North Church in Boston, was Increase Mather. Cotton was a scholar, taking notes of his father's sermons in Latin by the time he was eight years old. He is the youngest to enter Harvard, beginning his college education at eleven years old. He had the largest library in the new world at the time. He was fluent in Latin, Greek, and Hebrew, and he wrote over three hundred and fifty books. His most prominent book was *Magnalia Christi Americana,* an early history of the progress of the gospel in Puritan New England.[41] His first wife died, apparently from breast cancer. His second wife died after giving birth to twins during a measles epidemic in Boston. The twins died a few days later. By the end of his life only two of Mather's sixteen children had outlived him.

But what I wish to focus on now, something I hope will be an encouragement to you, is how he handled the trauma of the last ten years of his life. He married Lydia Lee George after his second wife died, and Lydia was a well-to-do, manipulative, worldly, and perhaps even psychopathic woman. She would fall into long periods of what Mather called *prodigious paroxysms,* berating him and his children. She even left him for a season. She eventually was reconciled to him. Then there was Mather's son, Creasy,

---

40. Silverman, *The Life and Times of Cotton Mather.*

41. Mather, *Magnalia Christi Americana* (*The Great Works of Christ in America,* Two volumes).

who held such promise as a scholar and pastor. By the time he was twenty, however, he gave up the idea of the ministry and became a sailor. He lived the kind of life for which sailors are notorious. He was even accused by a prostitute of fathering her child. This broke Mather's heart, and he fasted and prayed for the salvation of his son. Finally Mather received the devastating news that his son was lost at sea, apparently dying without coming to Christ. Then there was financial hardship. He became the executor of Lydia's estate that she acquired from her first husband when he died. He left a business of many assets and liabilities. Mather thought the assets were more than the liabilities, but soon was sued for debts not paid. Lydia refused to part with her own money to pay for her first husband's debts, plunging Cotton into near bankruptcy, bringing shame to him in the Boston community. He was wrongfully accused of not paying his debts. Yet in the midst of these hardships there is great evidence of profound joy and peace. How did he do it?

The text mentioned above gives insight into how we are to live in the midst of unrelenting hardship—the big three of marriage, money, and children. Do you sometimes feel trapped, incapable of excising yourself from unrelenting hardship and disappointment? Do you feel as though you live in an oppressive marriage or financial hardship? How about a child or two who is not walking with Christ, and you are burdened about his soul? What are you to do?

Paul tells us that he is praying for three things—that we may know the hope of His calling, the riches of the glory of His inheritance in the saints, and the surpassing greatness of His power toward us who believe. He says that the proof of our possession of these is Christ's resurrection from the dead, and His eternal session at the Father's right hand. He goes further to say that the result of such is His dominion over every created thing. Finally He says this dominion of Jesus is revealed in two overarching truths—the Lordship of Christ over creation, and His headship over the church, His body.

This phrase "the fullness of Him who fills all in all" is a controversial one for Biblical commentators. Some say we should interpret this as we, the body of Christ, filling up that which is lacking in Jesus. John Calvin and William Hendriksen hold that view, and there is some merit to it.[42] After all we are told that we fill up that which is lacking in Christ's afflic-

---

42. See John Calvin and William Hendriksen's commentaries on Ephesians. Both argue persuasively for this position.

tions, (Colossians 1:24). However the context, plus the passive nature of the participle here, seems to me to mean we should interpret this as Christ the head filling up all that is lacking in us, the body. In other words, as one commentator puts it—"we have all the divine power and qualities which Christ possesses, and thus we are pervaded with His presence, animated by His life, and filled with His graces."[43]

In other words, the remarkable and glorious truth, dear Christian, is that by virtue of your union with Christ through His death and resurrection, you have all that Jesus has. You have His divine power, (Colossians 1:27). Why then can you not live with great hope? You have His divine qualities, (2 Peter 1:3–4). Certainly I do not mean incommunicable attributes like eternity and omnipotence. However I do mean His communicable attributes like holiness, goodness, justice, and mercy. Why then can you not live on a higher level, not falling to the oppressive nature of your circumstances? You are pervaded with His presence, (Matthew 28:20). Why then can you not live with great peace? You are animated by His life, (John 17:22). Why must you live in despair?

Jesus makes a stunning request of His Father saying, "And the glory which Thou hast given Me I have given to them; that they may be one, just as We are one." Why then would you settle for so little in your life? You are filled with His graces, (Romans 8:10). Though your body is dead because of sin, meaning a seed of death that corrupts the physical body is at the heart of your physical being; it is still true that a seed of life is in your spiritual being through Christ's righteousness given to you. This means a true believer will progressively grow more and more into the likeness of Jesus Christ. Why then would you settle for things that at best are neutral and at worst harmful to you?

Dear believer, you can live above your oppressive circumstances, but to do so you must daily embrace Jesus by faith. How? Look at His word, His mighty acts in the gospels, meditate on what God says about Jesus. Believe what He says. Obey what He commands, and when you fail run back to Him in repentance. The certain fact of Christ filling up that which is lacking in you is the staggering reality that you are pervaded with His presence, animated by His life, and filled with His graces. To believe and act upon this proves you have eternal life. It proves you have a revival life.

---

43. Lenski, *Commentary on Ephesians*, 402, 403.

Resurrection Implications

And they went out and fled from the tomb,
for trembling and astonishment had gripped them;
and they said nothing to anyone, for they were afraid.

THE THREE WOMEN WHO came to the tomb that first Easter morning showed wonderful devotion to the Savior. When the disciples had scattered at His arrest, the women stood at the foot of the cross while Jesus was crucified. After He died they probably helped Joseph of Arimathea wash the body of Jesus, and began preparing it for burial. Since Jesus died around three p.m., and since it probably took another hour or so to receive permission from Pilate to receive the body, they were not able to finish the preparation for burial. That's because at sundown on Friday the Sabbath began, and no work could be done for twenty-four hours. So the women had to wait until Saturday at sundown to purchase more spices. Their intent was simply to preserve the body of Jesus from putrefaction for a few more days. They came to the tomb on that Sunday morning, waiting until daylight so that they could see what they were doing, in order to better prepare Jesus' body for burial. As women of supreme devotion to Jesus, they came to the tomb with both hope and unbelief. By hope I mean they were so intent on preserving the body of Jesus they had not really considered how they might roll the heavy stone away. They obviously were incapable of doing so. Nor had they thought about the Roman guard at the tomb, how they might get past it. Nonetheless their love for Jesus moved them forward to do a seemingly impossible task. But they were also filled with unbelief, and we know this because Jesus had told His disciples at least four times that He would be crucified, and three days later be raised from the dead. The thought of this actually happening was completely foreign to the minds of these devoted women. They were coming to prepare His body for burial. They were not expecting to see a resurrected Savior. When they came to the tomb they found the stone rolled away, and looking inside the tomb, found a man sitting, clothed in garments, whiter than white. He was saying to them, "Do not be amazed; you are looking for Jesus the Nazarene, who has been crucified. He has risen; He is not here; behold, here is the place where they laid Him. But go, tell His disciples and Peter, 'He is going before you into Galilee; there you will see Him, just as He said to you.'" The word "amazed", in some translations is rendered *afraid*. Actually the word has a very full meaning that is vitally important to our understanding of how we are to live in this world. They were afraid, awed, amazed, profoundly thankful, overjoyed. They were giving praise to God. The emotion they had was like one who narrowly escapes drowning, like one who is cured of a terminal illness by some new drug or procedure. They were like those on that U.S. Air flight that ditched into the Hudson River. All thought they were going to die, and then were amazed to find that all had survived. You will note also that after receiving this command from the angel, the women went immediately to the disciples, not speaking to anyone along the way. The resurrection of Christ, properly understood and applied, also brings obedience.

Many today are terribly confused about the nature of Christianity, and what the church is to do. Some think Christianity is a white man's religion, a western cultural phenomenon. Others think it is a political action committee for those on the right or left. Some think the church is for entertainment, for psychological well being, for social gatherings. Some are expecting things of the church that she cannot or should not try to do. But Christianity is the life of God in the soul of man, and the church's job is to do what no other organization can do—prepare people to live and die well. She is to point out the sinfulness of man, and God's only remedy through Christ's death and resurrection.

The unbeliever who sits in a worship service ought eventually to be disturbed, concerned, and troubled. I know how controversial this statement may sound to some people. After all, we should intensely desire for people to find the church a welcoming place. We ought to be friendly and inviting to all who enter her doors. But a church that is heavy on grace and light on law, a church that does not preach a discriminating message, where people know, after listening to a sermon that they are either in the kingdom or out of the kingdom; I suggest is not doing its job. To paraphrase John MacArthur from his book, *Ashamed of the Gospel*—an unbeliever who sits in church for more than a couple of weeks ought to be so uncomfortable that he does one of two things. He leaves out of fear or disgust at the message, or seeks Christ until he is assured of his salvation, his right standing with God.[44] The latter may take a long time, perhaps even years, but the gospel calls people to specific action. True gospel preaching eventually evokes one of two responses—true belief and repentance or rejection of Christ. The division over this issue in the modern American church can be traced back to the same theological issue of the second Great Awakening. The major players were Asahel Nettleton, a strong Calvinist who believed in the total depravity and inability of man to believe the gospel on his own efforts; and Charles Finney, an Arminian who believed man has the ability to believe the gospel without the Holy Spirit's regenerating work. These two preached in very different ways. This led to New School and Old School Presbyterianism[45] that is very much with us today in one form or another. One very popular author and pastor has said that anyone will come to Christ if the one sharing the gospel finds the key to his heart. This is Arminianism, and terribly discouraging to preachers. In other words, to follow this thinking all the way through—if you are not slick, winsome, and really understand how to speak to people, then you should not expect a whole lot from your evangelistic efforts.

But these women, seeing the empty tomb were filled with devotion, hope, joy, fear, terror, and rejoicing. They desired to obey God and to repent daily of sin. True Christian faith does this to people. Becoming a Christian will evoke a profound change. The truly converted begin to love God and hate their sin. They begin to believe that simple faith in Jesus can help them gain victory over their past sins that so enslaved them. They begin to glory in the cross of Christ. If you are not there, then it must be for one of two reasons. Either you never have been given new life in Christ, or you have lost your way from sincere devotion to Him. Repent and believe the gospel if the former. If the latter, then repent of your coldness of heart—for settling for lesser things, for doubting the power of Jesus to transform you and others. Open yourself to the Holy Spirit in prayer. Know and believe that if He chooses not to move on people, then there is nothing you can do to convince them. However you also need to believe that if He does draw one by the Spirit, there is nothing that unbeliever can

44. MacArthur, *Ashamed of the Gospel: When the Church Becomes Like the World.*

45. See Ahlstrom, *A Religious History of the American People,* volume 1, 551 for a succinct and accurate explanation of Old School and New School Presbyterianism.

do to stand against the regenerating work of God in his life. May we live with joy, hope, reverence, fear, and profound thanks to God! Tell others of the resurrection of Jesus, always depending upon the Holy Spirit to open people's eyes and ears, and sit back in profound wonder when He does it.

All You Need Is in Jesus

*... to be specific, that the Gentiles are fellow-heirs and fellow-members
of the body, and fellow-partakers of the promise in Christ Jesus
through the gospel.*

EPHESIANS 3:6

O N OUR CHURCH'S MISSION trip to Kampala, Uganda, we spent two
days in a slum called Kiefimbira, teaching a Bible Club for children
and distributing clothing to many mothers and grandmothers there.
Originally we counted twenty-five women at our meeting and put the
clothing in that number of piles. By the time we began distribution however, the number had doubled. We cut the piles as much as we could but
still many women did not receive any clothing for themselves or their
children. This was a vivid illustration to us. We can never satisfy all the
temporal and physical needs of the poor. This is not to say that we should
not show mercy and compassion to those in physical need. What was remarkable about this incident is how content these women seemed to be
with a gift of little or nothing. It seems that they have come to understand
something we need to learn—our needs are not primarily physical or
temporal. Instead they are eternal and spiritual.

Paul puts forth a remarkable three-fold declaration in this verse on
the standing of the Ephesian brethren who formerly were pagans. He declares that they are fellow heirs, fellow members of the body, and fellow
partakers of the promise in Christ Jesus through the gospel. Paul is in the
midst of a parenthetical statement (verses 2–13) where he is reiterating
the remarkable truth that the middle wall of separation between Jew and
Gentile is abolished through the death of Christ. What does Paul mean
by fellow heirs, fellow members of the body, and fellow partakers of the
promise? He means that these Gentiles are on equal footing with Jewish
believers who had far more privileges than they. They are beneficiaries of
the riches of God's eternal salvation (Ephesians 1:3–14), being made heirs

66

of God and fellow heirs with Christ, (see also Galatians 3:29, Romans 8:17). When Paul declares them to be fellow members of the body he uses a word never used elsewhere in the Greek New Testament. Furthermore, the word cannot be found in secular Greek writings of the day. This means that Paul probably coined the word himself. The idea is one Paul develops in other places (see 1 Corinthians 12, Ephesians 2:16) and it means that all believers in Christ, regardless of their nationality or ethnic or economic status, are in the spiritual body of Christ, that we are united to Him, that we are bone of His bone and flesh of His flesh, to borrow a phrase from John Calvin.[46] Finally Paul says that we are fellow partakers of the promise. What promise? The prophetic word of Genesis 3:15, Genesis 12:1–3, Psalm 2, Isaiah 7:14, Isaiah 9:6, 7, Jeremiah 31, among many others; is fulfilled in the first advent of Jesus Christ. In the fullness of time, God sent forth His Son who was born of a woman, born under the law, in order that He may redeem us from the works of the law (Galatians 4:4–6). In other words the Gentiles are partakers of the promise of Christ, just as the Jewish believers are.

Okay, that's the gist of the text, but what difference does this make in how we live? How does it move you to revival living? It drives home the glorious truth that *all you need is in Jesus Christ.* Therefore can you not put away the folly of lesser things? You think your greatest need is physical, financial, social, emotional, psychological, material, or temporal. You reason, "If only I had a better job, more money, a better spouse, children who obeyed me, then I know I would be content." You know you are thinking this way when these things take first place in your life. You know this is happening by observing how much they dominate your thoughts, emotions, words, time, and actions. I know you work forty to sixty hours weekly, but I suggest you can still put in these hours and not live for the temporal and material. You are buying into the temporal as the most important when you acquire wealth as an end in itself. Why are you working? Why are you saving and investing money? Be honest with yourself? Is it for your own comfort? Is it for your children? Is it for pleasure? There is nothing wrong with acquiring wealth, but the question is—why?

Your greatest need is spiritual and eternal, being in right relationship with God, knowing your sins are forgiven, knowing that He loves you

---

46. Calvin, *Commentary on Ephesians*, 160.

and will take you to heaven when you die. This need can only be met in Jesus Christ. That's the whole point of Paul's declaration in verse 6. Does this sound bigoted? What about all the religions of the world—Islam, Hinduism, Animism? The greatest sickness, being estranged from God, requires the greatest remedy. You were enemies of God. You hated God. You hated His attributes—things like His inexhaustible love, immutable goodness, unsearchable wisdom, unfathomable grace, unmitigated transcendence. You hated His law, His word. And you hated His people. This was true of you prior to your conversion. And you did so because you were dead in your sins. You were willing to thank people for kind deeds done for you, but you failed to thank God for His bountiful blessings to you. You were enamored with people of position and power, yet you failed to acknowledge or love the Creator and Sustainer of the universe. Such folly! However God was rich in mercy to you, opening your eyes to your sin and spiritual poverty, showing you Jesus, giving you faith to repent and believe His gospel. The fact is—all you need is in Jesus.

Can you not therefore, put away the folly of lesser things? Paul says in Philippians 3:18–19 that the earthly minded are enemies of the cross of Christ, that their end is destruction, that their god is their appetite, who glory in their shame. But if you are in Christ Jesus, if you are fellow heirs, fellow members of the body of Christ, if you are fellow partakers of the promise, then you are heavenly minded. Your citizenship is in heaven where you eagerly wait for the Savior, who will turn the body of your humble state into conformity with the body of His glory by the exertion of His power to subject all things to Himself.

I suggest our wealth and modernity are doing a number on us, seducing us to believe that our greatest needs are physical or temporal. God has done the Ugandans in Kiefimbira a huge favor. By depriving them of stuff, they are forced to run to Jesus for refuge. They have no other place to go. Your wealth gives you options that wage war on your soul. Your task is much more difficult that the people in Kiefimbira. You must suffer the hardship of worldly wealth. What is the remedy? Guard your heart and mind. What dominates your thinking, speech, time, emotions? What is the objective of wealth acquisition? Allow the Holy Spirit to show you improper priorities and repent in humility. Look at godly people, how they hold their stuff loosely. And look at Jesus, who though He was rich became poor for your sake. You will battle this until you die, but the battle is worth fighting. All you need is in Jesus. That is revival living.

You Are No Match for Your Enemies

. . . far above all rule and authority and power and dominion, and every name that is named, not only in this age, but also in the one to come.

EPHESIANS 1:21

JOHN GOODWIN, A BRICK mason living in Boston in 1689 had four young daughters given to bizarre behavior. When a pastor visited to pray with one of the young girls, she went deaf during his prayer; but when he finished, she was able to hear again. On another visit the pastor noted that all four girls appeared to swallow their tongues. They also opened their mouths exceedingly wide and then closed them rapidly like a spring lock. They also had hyper-extended elbows and knees and their bodies and faces were in extreme contortions. The pastor believed they were bewitched which eventually led to the trial, conviction, and execution of a woman in Boston as a witch. Three years later the same kind of bizarre things were happening in nearby Salem, eventually bringing the infamous Salem witch trials. The Puritan court executed nineteen women and one man for witchcraft.[47] Not one of the better moments of our Puritan forefathers.

Obviously I do not know if the Goodwin girls were bewitched, but there is no doubt that seen and unseen, natural and supernatural, material and immaterial forces of both good and evil are in this world, constantly vying for the eternal souls of men, women, and children. You are no match for these enemies. Perhaps you find yourself from time to time facing a very strong temptation to do evil, something so wicked and bizarre that after the initial delight in considering it, you are then repulsed by the thought. This, however, brought a sense of guilt and shame, perhaps even frustration to your heart. "How could I possibly consider such evil?"

47. Silverman, *The Life and Times of Cotton Mather,* 83ff.

We typically try to fight these enemies by reminding ourselves how much we will lose if we go there, how much shame this will bring to our spouse and children, how this will shame our Lord Jesus, how this will bring financial ruin to us. Consider this, dear Christian—if this is your method of fighting your enemies then you will eventually fail. These are not God's appointed way to fight sin. Eventually even these ideas and thoughts cannot stand up against the enemy and temptation. A woman will come along, for example, so attractive, so winsome that for a disastrous moment you will say, "I don't care what this will look like. I want her."

Pretty frightening stuff, isn't it? But I have good news for you. God has not left us without a means to fight our enemies. We have an exalted Christ who has dominion, due to His resurrection and session at the Father's right hand (Psalm 110:1, Hebrews 1:3, 1 Peter 3:22), over every created thing. No thing and no person, whether material or immaterial, visible or invisible, natural or supernatural can rival the dominion of Jesus, King of Kings and Lord of Lords.

What are those enemies you face and how do they work on you? I will briefly mention six of them. The first is Satan who, as a roaring lion, is always seeking those whom he may devour. He seeks to delude you, to make you think that repentance for sin is easy, always failing to tell you how enslaving sin will be. He brings confusion to you and your spouse, your children, your church. Sometimes in the midst of argument or strife you cannot even remember how it started. Then he loves to bring accusation, reminding you of what a loser and failure you are, how Christianity is not working for you, how you are unworthy of Christ's shed blood. Of course all these things are true about you, but the devil certainly does nothing to remind you of the remedy in Jesus. Two, guilt and shame, like that of Adam and Eve in Genesis 3 cause you to seek peace in creation rather than the Creator. This usually comes in the form of money, shopping, hobbies, or any other quest to build your self-esteem. Three, inward corruption constantly plagues you. You wonder sometimes how you can feel so close to God, and then five minutes later be given to lustful, wicked, hateful thoughts and speech. Your inward corruption is terribly frustrating and disconcerting. Indeed the very thing you wish to do you do not do. Four, ungodly influences and people abound to draw you away from Jesus. Proverbs warns constantly of bad friends, not to run with them. Five, trials and afflictions come and we wrongly interpret them, believing them to be payback time for previous sin, not realizing they are meant to sanctify us so that we may glorify God. And six, death, or at least the process of dying, frightens us, robbing us of the joyful expectancy of seeing Jesus face to face, (Hebrews 2:15).

But Jesus has dominion over all created things. How did He gain the victory? Consider these five actions—His incarnation (Colossians 1:15), His humiliation (Isaiah 53:10–11), His exaltation (Psalm 68:18–20), His work of regeneration, sanctification, and glorification in His people, and His providence where He directs and disposes all things for His own glory (Psalm 115:3).

This sounds like nice theology, but allow me to be much more practical. To overcome your enemies, you must put on Christ Jesus our Lord. You must regularly and consistently be meditating upon, thinking about the Lord Jesus, allowing the Holy Spirit to put within you a growing, experiential love for Him. I suggest you regularly go to the gospels and read the stories of Jesus' mighty works of healing and compassion. Read the stories existentially, as though you were there, as though you have never read them before. See what Jesus has done and then present arguments to yourself. You should argue from the greater to the lesser. For example, the healing by Jesus of the Gerasene demoniac in Mark 5 could bring you to say, "If Jesus could save and heal such a hopeless man, then surely He can help me." Or you may argue the lesser to the greater, "If God provides for the lilies of the field and for the birds, then surely He will provide for me, one for whom Jesus died."

Moralistic, self-improvement, self-discipline programs to defeat Satan, guilt and shame, inward corruption, ungodly influences from which you can never fully hide yourself, the consequences of afflictions and trials, and the fear of death will not work long term. You need Jesus if you are to live a revival life. Take Him daily by faith. Believe in what He says, who He is, and what He did, is doing, and will do. You have a Savior who knows no rival.

Forfeiting Your Freedom in Christ

. . . among them we too all formerly lived in the lusts of our flesh,
indulging the desires of the flesh and of the mind and were by nature
children of wrath, even as the rest.

EPHESIANS 2:3

ERNEST HEMINGWAY, AN AMERICAN icon of the twentieth century, one who perhaps more than any other writer, changed the way novels in the English language are written, had a strong evangelical upbringing. His grandfather was a graduate of Wheaton College, still today one of the bastions of evangelicalism. He was also the Director of the Chicago YMCA in the late nineteenth century. Hemingway's parents were strong believers as well. Ernest grew up in a home where family devotionals were held morning and evening, where church was central to his life, where he served as a leader in his youth ministry. But Ernest was looking for adventure and became an ambulance driver in World War I, later living in Paris, giving himself over to all manner of debauchery, denying the faith of his parents and grandparents. He became a great literary man, loved and admired by many, but his life was a mess. He was terribly unhappy and finally committed suicide in 1960. He had known the freedom of the Christian faith, but gave it up. What happened and why?

Hemingway no doubt knew the great truths of the Apostle Paul, recorded in Ephesians 2:1–10, but he allowed freedom in Christ to lead him into license. Be sure of this—you will never appreciate what you have until you understand what you deserve. Paul declares to them in Ephesians 2:3 that they had two things which characterized them prior to their conversion. First, they were living well ordered but chaotic lives apart from the Holy Spirit's presence and power. To live in the lusts of the flesh meant that their intense desire was to live apart from God. The Greek word we translate "lust" can mean good or evil desires, as in Luke 22 when Jesus said that He strongly desired to eat the Passover with His disciples.

But here Paul has in mind this all consuming passion to have what they wanted then, regardless of the consequences. "Flesh" here means life apart from God. Saul of Tarsus before his conversion, later becoming Paul the Apostle after meeting Jesus on the road to Damascus, comes to mind. Second, they were consistently, creatively indulging their wills. The Greek word, translated here as "indulging", is our root word for poem. It is also used in verse 10, "We are His workmanship." In other words, the Ephesians, as well as you and I, had our own very creative way of sinning. Paul does not use lust to describe this. Instead he uses the word "will", meaning we had a deliberate, well-considered, intentional, willful choice to pursue our own brand of sinning. This was manifest in two ways—the will of the flesh and mind. "Flesh" here means animalistic desires that are not necessarily sinful, at least in the beginning. God has given us natural desires for food, sleep, sex, drink, and physical exercise. However we can eat too much or too little. We can sleep too much or too little. We can pervert our natural, God-given desire for sexual intimacy through fornication, adultery, pornography, homosexuality, and all manner of variations on these. We have a natural desire for drink but we abuse it with alcohol and prescription or illegal drugs. We ought to take care of our bodies through regular exercise but we do too much or too little.

And then there is the creative, consistent indulgence of our wills in the use of our minds. This may be known in base, godless thinking like pride, envy, jealousy, bitterness, racial bigotry. But it may also be evident in more respectable thinking such as ambition, the desire to get ahead, to engage in self-improvement. And it may also be seen in good things like art, music, culture, movies, theatre, reading and thinking about our hobbies, home improvements, philosophy, history, even theology. It is one thing to satisfy natural desires that God has given, and it is not wrong to find enjoyment in the lawful pursuit of these and the higher thoughts coming from art, culture, and history; but it is quite another to become consumed by them, of being so dominated that they take our time, rob our affections, take us away from our spouse, children, and most importantly God.

In light of this well ordered but chaotic life in the lusts of the flesh, in light of our consistent indulgence of the wills of the flesh and mind, can you not see that God was perfectly just in declaring you a child of wrath? You were corrupt, like the sullied waste band of Jeremiah 13. You were totally worthless to God. Furthermore, your behavior was no better.

You were rebellious, stiff-necked against the God who had shown such kindness to you. "But God" . . . I love to remind people of the mercy and grace of God. You deserve hell. No doubt about it. But God was merciful. He sent His Son to die for you. He opened your eyes to see your sin, He gave you a new heart to repent and believe the good news of Jesus.

This means, dear believer, that you are free in Christ. You are set free from your former manner of life. Why then do you go back to slavery to sin? Why do you go back to an inordinate, perverted use of your flesh, seeking to satisfy your physical desires for food, sleep, sex, drink, and the care or abuse of your body? For one reason, and it is the same reason Hemingway forgot his Christian pedigree. At that particular moment, you loved your sin more than you did Jesus.

You are free in Christ Jesus, but this does not mean you are free to do whatever you wish. You are not free to neglect public worship. You are not free to neglect your familial duties. You are not free to not seek God in private devotion. You are not free to not tithe your time and money. But you are free to not do what you ought not to do. But how can you gain victory over your propensity to go back to slavery? When we put it like this, it all seems so silly to sin, does it not? The solution is always the same, and it is very simple, yet profound. Fall in love with Jesus, day after day. Think on your Savior. Read about Him in the gospels stories. Put yourself in the stories. I mean really think about what is happening. See the beauty and glory of Jesus. Ask the Spirit to rekindle your love for the Savior. When you walk about daily think on who He is and what He has done for you. Think on how He has delivered you from the condemnation you so justly and unquestionably deserve. See how He has come to you when you had no ability, no desire, no interest, no understanding. When you do then, at least for that moment, you will fall down in love and wonder before the God of all mercy. Now, repeat this process many, many times per day. And when you fail, and you certainly will fail, do it again. Oh, the depths of the riches, both of the wisdom and mercy of God!

Denying Jesus

Peter remembered how Jesus had made the remark to him,
"Before a cock crows twice, you will deny Me three times."

MARK 14:72

DURING THE PASSOVER MEAL Jesus warned His disciples that one of them would betray Him. Then, after giving them bread and a cup of wine, symbolizing His death for them, Jesus told them that all of them would fall away. He said that they would be scattered like sheep from their shepherd. Peter confidently said, "Even though all may fall away, yet I will not." After being told that he would deny Jesus three times, Peter said, "Even if I have to die with You, I will not deny You!" Later, in the Garden of Gethsemane, Judas came with a mob, wielding swords and clubs, to arrest Jesus. John tells us that Peter is the one who lopped off the ear of Malchus, the High Priests' servant. So, at least in the beginning, Peter showed a little courage, though terribly misguided. The rest of the disciples ran away like antelope when a lion attacks the herd. John tells us that Peter and an unnamed disciple (scholars speculate it was either Joseph of Arimathea or Nicodemus) were following far behind the mob as they led Jesus to Caiaphas, the High Priest. This unnamed disciple knew Caiaphas and was able to gain access to the High Priest's compound, Peter remaining momentarily outside until he was cleared to enter. As Peter was passing by a servant girl said, "You, too, were with Jesus, the Nazarene." Peter vehemently denied it. Peter then walked out on the porch, instinctively distancing himself from the crowd to remain as anonymous as possible. Matthew tells us that Peter sat down with the officials, waiting to see what would happen. What does this mean? Peter probably did not expect Jesus to die. He no doubt thought that He would somehow pass out of their midst, as He had done in John 8 and 10, when religious leaders were incensed at His words, planning to kill Him. A short time later the servant girl told those standing around the fire with Peter, warming their hands due to the cold temperature, that Peter was one of the followers of Jesus. Peter denied it again. This whole episode probably took several hours while Jesus is being interrogated on the inside by Caiaphas and the Jewish officials. Then the bystanders, who no doubt had been with Peter for several hours, perhaps engaging in rather jocular conversation, said to Peter, "Surely you are one of them, for you are a Galilean too." How did they know that? His Galilean accent no doubt gave him away. He was guilty by association. Peter then denied Jesus a third time, bringing down curses upon himself saying, "I don't know this fellow you are talking about." Peter then heard the cock crow a second time, and he wept bitterly.

Let's not be too hard on Peter. I bet you would have done the same thing. If you were living in Nazi Germany in the late 1930s, standing around speaking with a few SS soldiers, and one of them said to you, "Hey, I bet you are a Jew or at least a Jewish sympathizer. I saw you yesterday helping an old Jewish woman across the street." You would be terrified and deny any Jewish connection whatsoever.

But still, how could this happen to Peter? Not only did he have profound privileges, being with Jesus from the beginning of His ministry, witnessing all manner of healings, exorcisms, the feeding of the five thousand, walking on water, raising people from the dead, hearing remarkable preaching; but he was in Jesus' inner circle as an Apostle. He had confessed Jesus to be the Christ. He had witnessed Christ's transfiguration. He had been the recipient of special grace—the first to have his feet washed by Jesus, having prayer offered by Jesus when Satan asked permission to sift him like wheat. His pride, made manifest in his desire for self-preservation, is what got him.

Be sure of this—the seeds of denial are in you. If you are to live a revival life, then you must be clear on this. You must therefore be vigilant to guard your heart against pride for it can make shipwreck of your very best intentions. Peter did not plan on denying Christ, and neither do you. But you have denied Him, haven't you? How so? In at least three ways. First, you deny Jesus by outright, explicit refusal to speak to others about Him when given opportunity. You have friends, family members, neighbors, et al who need to hear about Jesus, and you remain in the guilty silence of self-preservation. Aren't you saying to your friends that you really don't care whether or not they go to hell! You may object by saying, "Wait a second, Al. Don't you believe in the doctrine of election? They are or are not going to be saved, and there is nothing I can do about it." True but the

Bible makes clear that God works through people to bring His gospel to the elect. Check out Romans 10:13–17 as only one example. Second, you deny Jesus by outright, explicit refusal to speak for Jesus to others. You are standing around the water cooler, and talk begins about the gay agenda, how Christians are hateful and mean spirited; and others are saying that the Bible is a book filled with hate because it condemns homosexuality. You stand there and say nothing. Or take the abortion issue. People are talking about how cruel and narrow minded Christians are for being against abortion and you say nothing. Or you hear people at a dinner party talking about how great the latest Elaine Pagels' book on the Gnostic gospels is, how wonderful it is to get another read on Jesus, and you refuse to call such talk heresy, refusing to speak for Jesus who is being impugned by this denial of His deity. And third, you deny Jesus when you act and speak one way at church, but quite another at work or with friends on the first tee. You are denying Jesus by your hypocrisy.

Well, what are you to do? You must acknowledge your guilty silence and hypocrisy as sin. Are you working off the root sin of pride, fearing for your own reputation? Are you yielding to the root sin of unbelief by failing to speak for Jesus, failing to trust Him with your name and job, fearing that you may lose both by saying what you know you ought to say? You must then repent, calling your behavior what it is—sin. You ought to be terribly devastated by your sin of cowardice. And then you must do what Peter did. Later, when Jesus was cooking breakfast for His disciples by the Sea of Galilee, Peter jumped into the water and made his way quickly to Jesus where He restored him.

Here's the beauty of the gospel, dear people. You are so much like Peter. In your pride and smugness you promise great things for Jesus but fail miserably, each and every day. He never grows tired, however, of restoring you when you repent. There is one other thing. Even after his restoration Peter still lacked Holy Ghost power. Only after receiving the baptism of the Holy Spirit at Pentecost did he have the boldness and efficacy in his preaching to affect real change. Put away your pride. Put away trust in your gifts, experience, planning, and training. Cast yourself daily on the Lord Jesus, believing in His presence and power. Then and only then will you be an effective witness for Christ.

Working Out Your Differences

There is one body and one Spirit, just as you were called in one hope of your calling, one Lord, one faith, one baptism.

EPHESIANS 4:4–5

WHAT IF JOHN WINTHROP[48] and Roger Williams had sat down, really listened to each other, putting aside all the divisive talk in the Colony? What if they humbled themselves before God and each other, and refused to separate, but stayed at it until they came to a mutual understanding and were able to coexist peaceably? What if a couple really listened to each other, saw their own sin, the idols of destruction bringing havoc in their family? What if they refused to divorce, no matter how painful and hopeless their circumstance seemed? What if they committed to work through their issues until reconciliation was reached? What if those so upset with the pastor's leadership style and preaching, those who drew conclusions about his motives without really listening to him, refused to leave the church, but instead insisted that all parties sit down at a negotiating table and work out their differences? What if parents who are estranged from a child refuse to allow the wall of separation to remain in their household? What if they refuse to give in to the iciness that pervades their home, instead insisting that they and the child sit down and talk things out until they understood each other, until all have repented and been reconciled? What if we would live out who we truly are, the one body of Christ, baptized by one Spirit into that body, all with one calling of hope for all eternity?

Doesn't it seem much easier simply to walk away from some relationships? Perhaps you have tried to talk with that difficult person and things became worse. Perhaps you are hurt from previous relationships

---

48. For a look at the problems between John Winthrop and Roger Williams, see Edmund S. Morgan, *Roger Williams: The Church and the State,* and Francis J. Bremer, *John Winthrop: America's Forgotten Founding Father.*

that have gone south, and you unconsciously avoid anything which may evoke similar feelings. Perhaps you have used the example of Paul and Barnabas' separation in Acts 15, because of a disagreement concerning John Mark, as the template of your separation, failing to realize that God never says their separation was a good thing.

Only a sadist revels in the possibility of confrontation and the hard work of reconciliation. This is really painful stuff, and that's why we avoid it so fervently. But the theological foundation is real. We are one body in Christ. He purchased us with His blood. He is the head and we are His body. If one part of the body is hurting, then the whole body suffers. This is a reality. You cannot deny Biblical truth. Your failure to reconcile with a spouse, child, church member, pastor, or some other brother or sister is harmful to the body of Christ. This is not revival living. This weakens the body, causing it to be susceptible to heresy, strife, loss of vision, and loss of resolve to take the gospel to the world. How many churches and families are absorbed with strife, not focusing on the big picture of living for Christ as His servants in the world?

Jesus prayed for the unity of His disciples in John 17:21ff, stating that they are one, even as He and the Father are one, so that the world may believe that the Father sent Him. This oneness does not ignore the real life issues of division, strife, and heresy. Jesus is not advocating peace at any price. He is not for a lowest common denominator theology, reducing faith to some nebulous idea that all religions are similar pathways to God. Nor is He suggesting that all division is bad. He tells His disciples in Matthew 7 not to judge, but then a few verses later He tells them to judge, to beware of the false prophets, to look at their fruit. He will separate the sheep from the goats on that great day. It may be that Jesus is not overly concerned about the preponderance of denominations in the world, especially when they began in response to the departure from orthodox theology. It may be that He considers some of them a necessity due to the weakness of our flesh, as He does divorce in certain circumstances.

But by unity He clears means the mystical, federal unity which now exists between Himself and all His blood bought people. We are in Christ. This is a theological declaration. (See Romans 6:1ff as only one example.) But there is a mystical unity as well. We really are part of Christ's body, and our job is to act like it. There is a basic, theological agreement with all believers in the world, regardless of their denomination, regardless of their worship styles and culture. At the very least, there is agreement on the Trinity, the two natures of Christ, the death and resurrection of Jesus Christ, the means of salvation which is through Jesus Christ alone by way of repentance and faith. This unity also means that we respect the practices and culture of those who name the name of Christ, though we may not particularly like the way they do church. This is not always easy. I once attended a community wide Concert of Prayer and the music ran the gamut. I walked into the meeting and rock and roll music in the name of Jesus was blasting from the speakers. I must say this really irritated me, but unity within the body of Christ means that I respect those who see it differently than me.

Let's be very practical here. Are you avoiding anyone? Have you given up discussion in your marriage or family and simply agreed mutually to coexist? Have you walked away from your church, or are you contemplating this, without trying to work out your differences with the pastor or leadership? Are you worshipping at the altar of comfort and ease, running from a problem relationship because it is the easy way out? What are you going to do the next time you have a problem relationship? Do you really think this will go away, that you will never need to confront such things again? Don't you think these relationships, at least for the sake of Christ and His Church, are worth saving? Don't you need this person in your life? Have you ever considered that God has brought this person into your life in order to show you your own sin, to reveal to you your sinful response, to make known to you your own idols? Have you forgotten that God is far more concerned about your holiness than your happiness? Have you failed to remember that God is sovereign in everything, that this problem relationship has not caught Him by surprise? Who are these people? Name them specifically. Now, what will you do? Remember the life of our Lord Jesus in this regard. In Luke 23:34, while dying for us on the cross, He cried out, "Father, forgive them for they do not know what they are doing." Jesus is not merely our example here, for we can never emulate His life. His life is a constant reminder of our failure to measure up to His standard. Rather by looking at Jesus who was able to forgive His murderers, we come better to understand that He now is our life, that we are indwelt with the living Christ by the Holy Spirit. This is our power to be reconciled to problem people. Will you believe this and act in faith?

The Danger of Inverted Priorities

Professing themselves to be wise, they became fools.

ROMANS 1:22

JOHN ADAMS, BORN AND reared in Braintree, Massachusetts, member of
the Continental Congress, Ambassador to France and Holland, negotia-
tor of the peace settlement with the British, ending the Revolutionary War,
the first Vice President of the United States, and the second President of
the United States, was from good Puritan and Calvinistic stock. His father
was a deacon in the Congregational Church of Braintree. John faithfully
attended church twice each Sunday and once per week for the weekly
lecture on Thursday. He remembered the preaching of George Whitefield
and Jonathan Edwards during the Great Awakening in his childhood. He
was a man of impeccable character, one given to sacrificing his health,
even the welfare of his family for the cause of independence. During a
period of fifteen years, beginning with the Continental Congress in 1774
until his election as Vice President in 1789, John Adams spent a total of
no more than two years with his family in Braintree. No one questioned
his zeal for the cause of freedom, and he paid dearly for it. His son Charles
became an alcoholic and John, in shame and embarrassment, disowned
him, not visiting him at all near the end of his life. John was given to prodigious outbursts of anger and rancor that were legendary. He also fought
times of depression, especially after losing his bid to Thomas Jefferson for
a second term as President in the election of 1800.[49]

By the time John had retired from politics and moved back to
Braintree, he was becoming increasingly skeptical of Christianity. He had
read in French the twelve volume *Origine de tous les cultes* by Despuis
that was a rationalistic, decidedly anti-Christian historical and philosophical survey of religion and superstition. He came out the other end a

---

49. McCullough, *John Adams*, 570.

confirmed skeptic, and when Jedediah Morse (the father of Samuel F. B. Morse from Midway, GA), an orthodox and Calvinistic Congregational pastor challenged the writings of William Ellery Channing and Adams' own pastor, Lemuel Briant, and their new ideas they called Unitarianism, John Adams came to their defense.[50] There is strong indication, therefore, that John Adams, who grew up in Calvinistic orthodoxy, died a Unitarian, skeptical of the Biblical faith. In fact when William Ellery Channing was called to be the pastor of the Federal Street Congregational Church in Boston in 1819 and confirmed in his sermon, what many had long suspected, John Adams was in his corner. Channing, like Adams, was a very kind and gracious man. Both were very moral and stood for many biblical values. However Adams followed Channing in the denial of the Trinity, the two natures of Christ, the doctrine of original sin, the imputation of Christ's righteousness, the reality of the devil and hell, and the necessity for the new birth.

Let this be a sober warning for all who read this. *Your theologically orthodox upbringing and church attendance alone will not keep you from error that can destroy your soul.* What happened to John Adams? Obviously I am speculating but could it be that two idols that took up residence in his heart, wrought irreparable harm? The first is the idol of notoriety. We know from Adams' early diaries that he was obsessed with making a name for himself. He longed for this more than anything. Second is the idol of busyness in a good cause. Who can argue with the importance Adams played in the beginning of our nation? He was an invaluable catalyst for the Revolution. But his busyness caused him to disregard his soul. He failed to attend the means of grace while in Philadelphia, Paris, Amsterdam, or Washington D.C. He no doubt, therefore, failed to read the Bible and pray in his private life. In other words, John Adams was terribly careless with his soul. So by the time he read Despuis he was so weak spiritually that he could not stand against the onslaught of skepticism and unbelief.

Don't think this could not happen to you? Perhaps a few questions are in order. What are the idols in your heart? You will act out, speak about what drives you. Your soul may be in trouble if you find little delight in, or desire for the glory of God. If you are more excited or thrilled by your work, your children, your money, or any other created thing than you are the prospect of standing in the presence of Jesus, then you are in trouble.

50. Ferling, *John Adams, A Life,* 433.

If you find it difficult to attend public worship, if you find the preaching of the word of God and public worship boring, if you are not filled up with Jesus, if you are not caught up in wonder, love, and praise at the beauty and majesty of Jesus, then your soul is in trouble. What's happening? You, like all people, are worshippers. You will always worship something. The question is—will you worship God or some created thing? Of course, if you are truly in Christ then the Holy Spirit will convict you of your sin, bringing you to repentance, preserving you from perdition. But don't presume upon God's grace. Watch over your heart with all diligence, for from it flows springs of life.

What's the solution? Don't be a fool. Don't ignore the overtures of God's grace to you. See your sin, your idolatry, and run back to Jesus, the lover of your soul, believing by faith the marvelous work he has done in your heart. Here's the word picture I often use. When you know you are not where you need to be, then picture yourself running from a swarm of bees pursuing you, running to a river, diving into it, in order to escape the pain of bee stings. This river, however, to which you are running, is filled with the blood of Jesus. See the danger to your soul, and run from your idols, forsaking them, plunging yourself afresh and anew into the river of grace, filled with blood, draw from the veins of Immanuel, our great God who is always with us. Be awed, amazed that God has come to you by the incarnation of His Son, that God entered our world and died for us. Always remember that Christianity is not a philosophy, not a mere teaching, not a moralistic alternative. It is the life of God in the soul of man, and when you again understand the implications of God's mercy in Christ, you will find your heart renewed, and your soul strangely warmed. This, alone, brings the revival life we all need.

Unity

. . . that they all may be one; even as Thou, Father, art in Me,
and I in Thee, that they also may be in Us;
that the world may believe that Thou didst send Me.

JOHN 17:21

T HE STRIFE, UNRESOLVED CONFLICT and tension, divorce, enmity
between parents and their children, division between brethren, and
church splits all deny a proclamation of unity in the body of Christ. In
Ephesians 2:11–16 the Apostle Paul lays down the theological foundation
for our spiritual union, proclaiming that the middle wall of partition has
been torn down by the Lord Jesus Christ in His reconciling death. He says
that the Gentile believer has been brought near by the blood of Christ.
He says that Christ, who is our peace, has made both groups into one by
abolishing in His flesh the enmity between Jew and Gentile. Paul makes
the same claim in Colossians 1:20 when he says that through Christ He
reconciles all things to Himself, having made peace through the blood
of His cross. And the prayer mentioned above by the Lord Jesus is not so
much asking the Father to bring unity as it is declaring the unity which
already exists between His disciples and those who would believe in Him
through their word.

As Martyn Lloyd-Jones points out in his exposition of this verse in
Growing In The Spirit [51] the unity that we now enjoy in Christ is not an
outward, organizational unity. It is not reducing religion or Christianity
to the lowest common denominator in order to gain consensus. It is not
a local ministerial association. It is not the ecumenical movement of the
World Council of Churches. And this unity does not deny the need, at
times, for new denominations or even church splits, due to theological or
doctrinal heterodoxy. But it is a unity founded on the unity in the Trinity,

51. Lloyd-Jones, *Growing in the Spirit: The Assurance of Salvation*, 133.

the essential oneness between the Father, Son, and Holy Spirit. Further, it is founded on the unity of the two natures of Christ, the so-called hypostatic union, where we acknowledge that Christ Jesus is fully God and fully man. Finally, it is established on the unity between all believers and the Lord Jesus. "We are buried with Him through baptism into death, in order that as Christ was raised from the dead through the glory of the Father, so we too might walk in newness of life," (Romans 6:4). In other words, we don't need to work up some nice feeling about unity. We don't need to compromise theology in order to gain unity. We already have unity with every believer in the world, regardless of his denomination, regardless of whether or not the secondary and tertiary dimensions of his theology line up with ours, and regardless of whether or not we choose to act on that unity.

Here's what I mean. I bet you have been in another part of our country or world, and met someone from an entirely different culture and you immediately connected with that person. You just knew you two were kin. You knew you were brothers and sisters in Christ Jesus. And on the other hand, you have met people who tell you that they are good Presbyterians, good Baptists, or whatever, and you do not sense the oneness of fellowship. What is going on there? The unity we have in Christ is an organic, inward, mystical unity, not necessarily an outward, organization, denominational one.

So, if you have any unresolved tension or conflict, any division or strife in your marriage, with your children, with your church or any other church, then you are effectively denying the organic unity of the body of Christ.

Though we have this organic unity it is possible to undermine it in the real world. How? You are tearing the unity of the body of Christ when you take away anything of the gospel essentials. If you, in order to gain a consensus from other churches or pastors, deny, for example, the exclusivity of Christ as the only means of salvation, then you are hurting the unity of the body. You can hinder that unity by adding to the gospel. When you agree that the Virgin Mary can be worshiped, or when you say, "Christ plus anything", then you are in trouble with disunity. You can hinder unity when you major on secondary or tertiary issues like baptism, election, church polity, speaking in tongues, etc. And you can bring disunity in the body of Christ by sinful behavior, working for your own agenda, bringing strife and discord to a church or family by sinful speech.

Are you moving toward a positive application of our essential unity in Christ, or are you contributing to disunity? Are you in tension or strife with anyone? Are you addressing this, working through it with the person, or are you avoiding the issue? If you are failing then here's why. It is because your heart is given over to idolatry.

What must you do? True revival living will never come in the face of disunity within the body of Christ. You need to deal very honestly with your idolatry, confessing it as sin, and forsaking it. How do you do that? Well consider the Lord Jesus Christ. We often consider the incarnation of Christ at Christmas time, and indeed it is right to do so, but the incarnation of Christ is far more than a nice Christmas story. John 1:14 tells us that God ripped open the heavens and came down, not unlike that for which Isaiah was praying in Isaiah 64:1ff. God ripped open heaven and stepped into our world in human flesh, enabling people to see the glory of God incarnate, dwelling amongst us with grace and truth. Grace refers to His favor bestowed on His people, enabling them to live for Him, to love their enemies, to pray for those who persecute them. Truth refers to the very essence of who He is, the God who cannot lie, who is utterly incapable of leading anyone astray. The incarnate Christ lived a perfect life, performing countless miracles, preaching powerful, life changing sermons. He raised people from the dead, He cast out demons, He healed people of disease. Finally He was arrested, falsely accused, beaten and scourged, being nailed to a cross between two thieves, dying a shameful death. Yet while on the cross Jesus said, "Father, forgive them for they do not know what they are doing." Jesus forgave those who wrongfully and cruelly crucified Him.

I am not asking you to try to do better and live by Jesus' example of forgiveness for you cannot possibly imitate Jesus. You are still prone to do evil because of indwelling sin. But I am asking you to live by faith, to realize that this same Jesus who prayed, "Father forgive them," is the same Jesus who lives within you by the Holy Spirit. You are to live by faith, looking to the resurrected and exalted Christ to give you power to strive for unity in the body of Christ.

Prevailing Against the World, the Flesh, and the Devil

. . . in whom the whole building, being fitted together is growing into a holy temple in the Lord; in whom you also are being built together into a dwelling of God in the Spirit.

EPHESIANS 2:21–22

IN 1555 THERE WERE five Protestant Churches in France. John Calvin, the French theologian and pastor of Geneva, was deeply burdened for his country, and was preaching, teaching, and sending young French preachers back there to plant churches. Within seven years there were over two thousand Protestant and Reformed Churches in France with a total membership of over three million people, fifteen percent of France's total population at the time. This growth was clearly a revival or awakening of remarkable size.[52] Queen Catherine de Medici was alarmed at this development, and stepped up persecution of the Huguenots, as they were called. She eventually drove many of them to Eastern Europe, America, and South Africa. Calvin and his followers knew that the normal Christian life was a fight, a spiritual battle against the world, the flesh, and the devil. How would they fight this battle? How should you fight it?

Paul, in the passage noted above, is making a staggering and profound declaration. He is telling these formerly pagan, godless Gentiles that they are now the holy temple of God. Paul uses a present participle and two present tense verbs in his declaration. He proclaims, he tells them that they are a work in progress. One does not build a temple in a day, a week, a month, or a year.

This truth ought to be a wonderful encouragement for every believer who feels he is losing the battle against the world, the flesh, and the devil. We know from what Paul says in Ephesians 2:14ff that Christ by His death has abolished, rendered powerless, the enmity that existed between Jew

---

52. McGrath, *Christianity: An Introduction*, 228.

and Gentile. We know from Colossians 1:15ff that Christ's death has re-moved our alienation from God, giving us peace with Christ. The Lord Jesus, therefore, is constantly, progressively building up His people to be the temple of God. Another way of saying this is that Christ Jesus, by the Holy Spirit, is prevailing against the world, the flesh, and the devil.

The Apostle John tells us to not love the world, nor the things of the world—the lusts of the flesh, the lust of the eyes, and the boastful pride of life, (1 John 2:15). Paul tells us to not give the devil an opportunity, (Ephesians 4:27). I like to describe these things by cities that seem to rep-resent them. Take the world, for example. It represents life without God, the idea that all is well, that we ought not to worry about the consequences of our actions. It says that now is all that matters. Las Vegas represents the world. You probably have heard the television commercial, urging us to spend our money in Las Vegas, "What you do here, stays here." Then there is the flesh, living for image, the sensual, a life given over to excessive exercise, dieting, and cosmetic surgery. The flesh is Hollywood. The devil is a deceiver, one who blinds the minds of the unbelieving so that they do not see the glory of God in Christ Jesus. Consider Salt Lake City, the headquarters of the Mormon Church, which works so hard at to convince an unknowing populace that she deserves to be called a Christian church, while clearly denying the deity of Christ and grace alone, through faith alone, through Christ alone as the only means of salvation. To embrace Las Vegas, Hollywood, or Salt Lake City is to convince yourself that ignor-ing the consequences of your actions is no big deal. It seeks to convince you to embrace the temporal, the physical, the sensual; and it convinces you to postpone the inevitable, giving account before a Holy God who will by no means leave the guilty unpunished. The result of celebrating Las Vegas, Hollywood, or Salt Lake City is to blind the lost so that they cannot see Jesus. To imbibe of these also weakens the resolve of believers, causing them to doubt the sufficiency of Jesus. In the end celebrating the world, the flesh, and the devil populates hell.

But I want to encourage you who are being built up as the holy tem-ple of God. Christ Jesus, who now resides in glory in the New Jerusalem, is constantly prevailing against Las Vegas, Hollywood, and Salt Lake City. How? Not by military, political, or economic might, but by the word of God and the Spirit. Paul says that the weapons of our warfare are not of the flesh, but divinely powerful for the destruction of fortresses, and we are destroying speculations and every lofty thing raised up against the knowledge of God and we are taking every thought captive to the obedience of Christ, (2 Corinthians 10:4–5). He tears down the walled cities of unbelief—Las Vegas, Hollywood, and Salt Lake City—by the ministry of the word of God through the power of the Holy Spirit.

The result of such ministry is a progressive subduing of the flesh (Galatians 5:16) so we slowly and consistently see progress in holiness. We find the devil being bound between Christ's first and second advents, so that Christ by the gospel is plundering the devil's house, taking captive those of the world, transforming them into growing, effective disciples. And Christ is presently conquering the world, making real the prophetic word from Revelation 11:15, "The kingdom of this world has become the kingdom of our Lord, and of His Christ; and He will reign forever and ever."

So, since these things are true of every believer in Jesus, can you not therefore live with a sense of hope and confidence, putting away your tendency for doubt or despair? How is Christ Jesus building you up? He does it by the work of the Holy Spirit in regeneration, conversion, sanctification, and revival. To be sure, you have a responsibility in holiness. I have spoken many times about this, but I wish now to focus on the certainty of Christ prevailing against the world, the flesh, and the devil in the believer's life. I know—you are not where you ought to be. You are not making the progress you should, but Christ does not build His temple in a day, month, or year. This is a long term construction project, one that He will not complete in you until He takes you to His heavenly Jerusalem. So be encouraged and marvel at what God is doing. Sometimes you are so close to the action that you cannot objectively see the progress you are making.

The Prisoner of Christ Jesus

For this reason I, Paul, the prisoner of Christ Jesus.

EPHESIANS 3:1

ADMIRAL GASPARD DE COLIGNY, military and naval hero of sixteenth century France, who had converted to the Protestant faith during the awakening in France in the 1550's, was in Paris in August 1572 for the wedding of Henry of Navarre, a Protestant, to Marguerite de Valois, a Catholic. Queen Mother Catherine de Medici had orchestrated this wedding in hopes of bringing peace to an increasingly volatile France. The Huguenots or French Protestants were flexing their muscles, causing no small concern on the part of the Roman Catholic hierarchy in France. Coligny was very close to King Charles IX, and his desire to move France toward support of the Netherlands against Spain incensed Catherine. Something had to be done. She sought to have Coligny assassinated, and when the attempt failed she knew that she must strike quickly before the Huguenots moved in revenge. On the night of St. Bartholomew's day, August 24, 1572, she sent her army against the Huguenots, murdering Coligny in his hotel room, and gathering up Huguenot men in the courtyard of the Louvre. She murdered them there. The killing continued for several more weeks, and between three thousand and five thousand Huguenots were murdered by Catherine's men. She effectively broke the back of the Protestant movement in France, something from which the country has never recovered, much to their own spiritual demise.[53]

Here's my question—if God loved the Huguenots, people for whom Christ died, those who were seeking to honor Christ in their lives, then why would He allow this to happen to His people? If God is all powerful, then why did He not intervene on their behalf? Let's bring this concept closer to home. In the last one hundred years more have died for their

---

53. Gray, *The French Huguenots: Anatomy of Courage*, 132ff.

Christian faith than the first nineteen hundred years of the church combined. If God loves the Christians of Sudan, Uganda, North Korea, Iran,
then why does He allow them to suffer? Why doesn't He intervene? And
even closer to home—as you consider the suffering and hardship of your
past or present, if God loves you, if God is all powerful, then why doesn't
He do something to prevent it?

The answer to these questions is seen in the words of the Apostle
Paul in the verse under our consideration. Paul refers to himself, not as a
prisoner of Nero, the Roman Emperor of the time who imprisoned him in
Rome; but as a prisoner of Christ. Surely Paul was a prisoner of Nero, but
he chose to look beyond his obvious and present circumstances. He saw
God in his suffering and hardship. He understood what God was doing,
for in Philippians 1:12ff he says that his imprisonment in the cause of
Christ has become well known throughout the whole praetorian guard
and to everyone else, and that due to his imprisonment most of the brethren had far more courage to speak the word of God without fear.

The simple, direct teaching of Scripture is that suffering and hardship are a reality for all believers. Consider some of the biblical data on
the topic. In Micah 5:1 the prophet is telling those in the northern kingdom, who face the threat of the Assyrian invasion, to muster troops for
their city was soon to be under siege, that with a rod they would smite
the Judge of Israel on the cheek. This clearly is a prophetic word, not only
to the present Judge of Israel, but to the Suffering Servant, the Lord Jesus
Christ, who would die for His people, (see Isaiah 42:1–3, 53:4–6). Paul
says in 1 Corinthians 4:9 that he and the other apostles have the sentence
of death upon them because they have become a spectacle to the world.
And Paul says in Romans 8:17 that though we are heirs of God and fellow
heirs with Christ Jesus, we also will suffer with Christ. So suffering is a
reality for Jesus, His apostles, and all His people.

To be more specific, God allows His people to suffer. The fall into
sin, stated in Genesis 3:17ff, makes clear that the earth has been cursed,
meaning things die, break down. Tornadoes, earthquakes, hurricanes,
genocide, wars, and pestilence all happen. In Philippians 1:29 Paul tells
the believers that for Christ's sake they were made not only to believe the
gospel but also to suffer for His sake. God allows His people to suffer. To
go further, however, we must also say that God brings suffering. Amos
3:6 says, "When a trumpet sounds in a city, do not the people tremble;
and when calamity occurs in a city, has not the Lord done it?" Isaiah tells

us that there is no other than God, the One forming light and creating darkness, causing well being and creating calamity. But to go even further, we must say that God also foreordains suffering and hardship. In Isaiah 46:9–11 we read, "My purpose will be established, and I will accomplish all my good pleasure . . . truly I have spoken, truly I will bring it to pass. I have planned it, surely I will do it."

But how do we put God's foreordination and eternal decree in place with man's obvious human ability to make decisions? We know man is not a robot. We know man is responsible for his own actions. The *Westminster Confession of Faith* says that God's eternal decree falls out, in His providence, by secondary means necessarily, freely, and contingently.[54] Consider this illustration to help you understand the concept. A plane that crashes, killing everyone on board, does not catch God by surprise. The only real comfort, the only thing that gives a sense of purpose for such a seemingly random act is that God allowed it, brought it, and foreordained it. But it happens through secondary means. A plane necessarily (due to the fall of mankind into sin that brings problems and malfunctions to everything) experiences at times mechanical failure, pilot error, or falls victim to weather problems. A plane contingently, due to the law of aerodynamics, when losing speed on takeoff, will begin to fall. Due to its speed upon impact, those inside the plane will die. But God did not make anyone who died in the crash get on the plane. They were free to make their own decisions. This is a mystery of what theologians call concurrence, the mysterious working of God's eternal decree and human responsibility.

But why does God allow, bring, and foreordain suffering and hardship? For at least three reasons—for the manifestation of His glory, the sanctification of His church, and the salvation of His elect. You need to step back, survey your situation, as Paul did in the Roman prison, and understand that God is always with you. You are a prisoner of Christ Jesus. He will be with you when you pass through the deep waters. How glorious would it be if all God's people lived out these glorious truths!

---

54. *Westminster Confession of Faith*, chapter 5, paragraph 2.

Trifling with Jesus

But they paid no attention and went their way.

MATTHEW 22:5

HORACE BUSHNELL, THE NINETEENTH century Congregational minister from Hartford, along with Universalist Hosea Ballou, and Unitarian William Ellery Channing altered the way many people thought about Christ's atonement. Until that time, the conventional view in the church of Christ was God-centered and objective.[55] That is, the sovereign Triune God who created man requires obedience from mankind. Due to man's fall into sin all are born with original sin and commit actual sin. Due to the infinite nature of that sin, man who has resisted the overtures of God's grace is under just condemnation for it. Death in this unconverted state means eternity in hell. Christ died to save sinners. His death satisfies the divine justice of God, thus removing man's just condemnation. This view of Christ's death is what theologians call the penal, substitutionary view of the atonement.

Bushnell, Ballou, and Channing all thought this a barbaric, uncivilized view of Christ's death. They doubted or denied the doctrine of original sin, and they equated sin with lack of knowledge. They therefore denied the infinite nature of sin. They taught that God would certainly not punish people infinitely by sending them to hell. Their view was that Christ shows the world God's love for people. Thus God longs to have people fellowship with Him. By admiring Christ's death men can be inspired to live such lives of sacrifice, even ridicule, for the good of others. This subjective, sentimental view of Christ's atonement is the prevailing view in liberal, New England churches to this day. This view also is prominent in evangelical churches throughout our nation. Does this shock you? I am not saying that evangelical pastors consciously and knowingly preach this

55. Douglas, *The Feminization of American Culture*, 125ff.

93

subjective, sentimental atonement, but I am suggesting that many do so in practice. It goes something like this, "God loves you and wants you to be part of His family and He wants you to live a prosperous and happy life. Come to Jesus for His death shows you how much God loves you and wants to bless you." In practice many therefore say, "Come to Jesus. He can help you get a date . . . He can help you feel better about yourself . . . He can help you become wealthy and buy a bigger house and a motor home . . . He can help you lose weight and become physically fit . . . ."

I am not denying that God helps people in many of these things, and I am not denying the glory of God's love for us, but a focus on these things misses the very point of Christ's atoning work. The prevailing view today is sentimental and subjective, man-centered, and it caters to the modern American ethos of rugged individualism and self-actualization. I suggest this drives the theology of many evangelical mega-churches in our country. We will not get revival from this kind of theology. The old idea of a penal, substitutionary atonement that focuses on the objective truth of man's condemnation and the satisfaction of it by the blood of Christ, is largely unknown today, much to the detriment of those within and without the church.

Bushnell, Ballou, and Channing have trifled with Jesus, and many following in their train have done the same. In the parable of Matthew 22:1ff, Jesus tells the story of a king who sends out his messengers to invite people to his son's great wedding feast, obviously a picture of the wedding feast of the Lamb in Revelation 19. The messengers go out into the surrounding towns, inviting people to the feast, telling them the fattened livestock have been prepared. But the people paid them no mind. They blew them off. They trifled with the invitation. Later we are told that those who would not come were cast into outer darkness. It is a troubling thing to trifle with Jesus. It is a damning thing to alter the teaching of Scripture on anything, especially something of eternal significance like the atonement.

Clearly Jesus has unbelievers in mind who have rejected the free offer of the gospel, who in their smugness and self-complacency see no need for Him; but can we not also make an application to those of us who are in Christ Jesus? Are you trifling with Jesus? What do I mean? Well, consider this analogy. You were a rebel, fighting against the Great King who finally conquered you and your nation. He gave you the terms of your surrender and you willingly submitted to Him. He took you in and gave you a place of prominence in His kingdom. He met your every need and then some. He protected you and provided for you and your family, only asking that you serve Him unreservedly. You knew that you owed everything, including your life, to this kind, benevolent King. In that context, you found your heart welling up with joy and gratitude for Him. You so enjoyed your times of communication with Him. You would wait expectantly for Him to come to you, and when He wrote you letters you poured over every word, quickly and willingly obeying His every command. You were motivated to make Him known to your friends and family members. You never grew weary of speaking of His kindness to you. There were times when you openly wept at His goodness, and when you disappointed Him, you were devastated and could not allow the estrangement to go long. You valued His calling on your life more than anything, willingly and freely giving your time, money, and heart to whatever cause He put before you.

However, after being in His kingdom for a number of years, you found that you were increasingly cold and indifferent to His communication and fellowship. You became careless in your obedience to Him. More frequently than not you were saying and doing things of which He disapproved. You no longer were troubled by your disobedience. And then you found yourself, at times, being outright rebellious toward Him, consciously and willfully disobeying Him, convincing yourself that He did not care for you or have your best interests in His heart.

Does this presently describe you? Are you trifling with Jesus? Are you paying no attention to His overtures of grace toward you? Perhaps you do not consciously deny the penal atonement like Bushnell, Ballou, or Channing; but do you practically deny it by failing to give your supreme affections to Him? Do you go long periods of time without praying to Him, without reading His word? Do you trifle with Jesus by placing your supreme affections on making money, your family, your hobbies, or your next trip?

What are you to do? You must first see that you are terribly guilty of trifling with Him, and then you must repent. Then marvel at His grace to you. How? Remember what you were. You were dead in your trespasses and sins. (See Ephesians 2:1–3.) You really were headed for an eternity in hell because you were guilty of flagrant disobedience to the One whose eyes are a flame of fire. But He had mercy. He shed His blood for you.

A Case for a Little Modern Day Chivalry

Let your statement be "Yes, yes", or "No, no";
and anything beyond these is of evil.

MATTHEW 5:37

RAOUL DE GAUCOURT, THE French captain who stood against the English and Henry V at their siege of Harfleur on their way to Calais, was captured by the English and then released, giving his word that he would later report back to Henry at Calais. On their way to Calais, Henry and his band of brothers encountered a French army five to ten times larger than their own at Agincourt, and defeated them in October 1415. On the exact day promised, Raoul de Gaucourt, along with twenty-five other French nobles turned themselves into Henry. Louis de Bourbon was captured at the battle of Agincourt, and was likewise taken into captivity and transported to London. Raoul de Gaucourt was finally released ten years later and served the French army until his death, some forty years later. Louis never was given his freedom. He was allowed to go back to France in order to meet obligations for his release by Henry V, including the need to raise a ransom the equivalent today of eleven million dollars. During his time in France Henry V died, yet Louis returned to England to serve as a prisoner, when he was not able to meet Henry's stipulations. He died in England and was buried there.[56]

Why would these men go to such extremes? After all, they denied Henry's claim to the French crown. They believed they were defending their country. They had wives and children. What made them honor their word? To answer this one must understand the cultural ethos of medieval Europe. Chivalry reigned supreme. Chivalry, from the French word *chevalerie,* or the English *cavalier*, referred to gallant knights or gentlemen, a system of knighthood where character qualities such as courage, nobility,

---

56. Barker, *Agincourt: Henry V and the Battle that Made England*, 352.

fairness, courtesy, respect for women, protection of the poor, and honoring one's word were practiced. A chivalrous man would do what he said he would do because his word was his honor. A French or English knight would never dream of breaking his word, let alone a vow.

Today, however, a man's word rarely means anything. Take vows, for example. Men and women take vows in marriage yet many easily discard them, especially when a better looking woman comes along, or when one's husband is too neglectful of the wife's needs. People take vows to submit to the leadership of their church, to support the church in her worship and work; but when a new preacher comes who people do not like, or when some other more exciting church catches their attention, then many members do not think twice about walking away, thus violating their church vow, made in the presence of God. Then elders in churches do the same thing, and their guilt is even more severe because they vowed before God to shepherd the flock of God under their charge. They walk away from their vow because they don't like the way things are going. How can we ever expect God to pour out His Spirit, and bring revival to His church when we live this way?

How can Christian people so easily break their vows, fail to honor their word? May I suggest three reasons? First, they do not take seriously what God says. Jesus said, "Say 'Yes, yes or No, no,' and anything beyond these is of evil." Solomon said, "It is better that you should not vow than that you should vow and not pay," (Ecclesiastes 5:5). In other words, if you are not sure you want to get married then don't take marital vows. If you are not sure about a particular church, then don't join it by making a membership vow. If you are not sure you can support your church, no matter what happens (unless there are doctrinal or other grievous sin issues not being addressed by the church courts), then don't become a deacon or elder. Second, they have far too low a view of the God who bought them with the blood of His Son. He is a covenant keeping God, who always does what He promises. They forget they are united to such a consuming fire, and that they will stand before Him, giving an account of their actions. And third, they have far too high a view of themselves. They convince themselves that though they took a vow, their circumstances are so unique and they are so important, that they are not really held to vows like other people.

Let's get specific. Did you take a marriage vow? You know what it was. Why not read over it again. Are you honoring it, or are you convincing yourself that in your unusual and difficult circumstances, it no longer applies to you? What about business contracts, or even your word on the performance of some product? Have you delivered the goods? Louis de Bourbon and Raoul de Gaucourt would never dream of not honoring their word. What about your vow of church membership? Is it not appalling today to see how people church hop? When one church seems more exciting, better programs, better preacher, more for the kids, they so easily throw away their vows to go to the hot spot. Have you left a church recently? Why? I am not saying there are never reasons to leave one, but are you violating your membership vow? What do you think this says to your children about fidelity to your word? And Ruling Elders and Deacons, who walk away from the flock of God under their charge—how can you so easily do it? Why did you take a vow if you are unwilling to keep it?

Our world desperately needs people of their word. We need men and women who will live out the revival life. You may think certain people are to be envied because of their success, but one day you will find yourself remembering and appreciating those who perhaps did not have much earthly success, but who now stand before your mind as giants of faith and integrity. Do you have eyes to see the significance of integrity, of modern day chivalry?

Can we practice a little chivalry? Can we take seriously the importance of saying "Yes, yes" or "No, no?"

Watch Where You Walk

Be careful how you walk, not as unwise men, but as wise.

EPHESIANS 5:15

WHEN I WAS FOURTEEN we made a trip to south Alabama to visit my father's uncle who lived in the country. We decided on that hot, muggy July day to go fishing. My father's uncle knew all the great spots, so I was surprised when he took us to a cow pasture. "Where's the lake?" I asked. It was in a clump of trees in the pasture, and as we entered into the cool shade of the small pond there were at least ten water moccasins on various felled trees at the water's edge. They would periodically slither off the trees and scoot across the top of the water. I noticed that my father had broken out into a cold sweat, and I was not too comfortable either. Finally when a water moccasin slid right beside my right foot into the water we had had enough. Wisdom dictated that we let the snakes have the pond. As we walked out of the woods you can bet we were very careful where we placed our feet.

Paul is telling us to be careful where we walk, to be vigilant in how we live. The *King James Version* says we are to walk circumspectly, like the police knocking down the door of a crack house who, with guns drawn, are looking in all directions for trouble. A pastor's greatest sorrow is to see people making poor decisions, sinful ones, knowing that such will bring destruction to them. We know this because we have seen it far too many times already. We can warn them, but so seldom do people listen. You are no match for the devil and your flesh. You are prone to folly, to act like a proverbial fool, one who refuses sound, Biblical advice. What should you do? How can you watch where you walk? How can you live a revival life?

I suggest three things, drawn from Ephesians 5:15–17. *First, you need to know the truth and apply the truth.* Paul says in verse 17 that we are to understand what the will of the Lord is. This is more than knowledge. This includes application. You need to reject worldly wisdom. The Jews sought

99

for signs and the Greeks sought for wisdom, but Paul preached Christ crucified. The Jews, who had seen countless miracles by Jesus, still told Him
that they needed more signs, to know whether or not He was the Christ.
People today seem to want more signs. They know of Jesus' miracles but
they want to see more of them. There is no need for them. What He has
recorded in Scripture ought to be enough. And the Greeks were steeped
in the philosophy of Plato, Aristotle, and Socrates. Paul rejected the temptation to appeal to the Greeks philosophically. Instead he preached Christ
to them as the only remedy for their sin. Today people seek the wisdom
of the world in many ways. Proverbs consistently tells us to use the rod
to discipline our children yet we tend to listen to godless child psycholo-
gists who tell us that spanking ruins a child's self-esteem. God says that
we have everything we need for life and godliness yet we tend to look to
psychiatrists to heal our spiritual and emotional problems.

It is also vital that you remember knowledge is never enough. Paul
says that knowledge makes proud, but love edifies, (1 Corinthians 8:1).
Knowing Reformed and Evangelical theology is a good thing, but some of
the meanest people I have known are solidly Reformed in their theology.
I have known Reformed adulterers, Reformed child abusers, Reformed
wife beaters, Reformed pedophiles, Reformed thieves, Reformed liars.
Hell no doubt is full of Reformed and Presbyterian people. If you are to
walk carefully in this world, keeping yourself from danger, then you need
to see things as they really are. Don't buy into the notion that man is basically good. That's not what the Bible says. It says that the throat of unbelievers is an open grave (the stench of rotting corpses is lodged in their
throats), that the poison of snakes is under their lips (the deadly poison
of king cobras waiting for the opportune time to strike you), that they
deceive with their tongues (I have in mind college professors who strip
unsuspecting Christian young people of their faith by mocking the Bible),
that their mouths are full of cursing and bitterness. So, your very nice,
non-Christian neighbor is at best filled with common grace which is no
better than embalming fluid which cannot give life. It can only preserve
a dead body from putrefaction for a time. And then you need to be clear
of who you are. Yes, you are made in God's image and you are in Christ,
but you also have within you conflicting desires, the flesh and the Spirit,
what I call the pig and the lion. The lion is the Lord Jesus, the Lion of the
Tribe of Judah. The pig is indwelling sin, your flesh, which has a voracious
appetite for garbage. A pig will eat anything while a lion only eats meat.

So you need to feed the lion and starve the pig. You need to take into your mind things that edify, not those things that enslave and destroy.

Second, if you are to walk carefully you also need not to waste your time. Paul tells us to buy up (like a stock broker who quickly buys up under-valued stock) the special time God gives us because the days are evil. Life in this world is fraught with danger, and you need to use your time wisely to strengthen you. Good is always the enemy of better, and better is always the enemy of best. It is good that you love your spouse and children, and it is better that you attend church regularly, but it is best that you lead your wife and children, that you teach them the Scriptures, that you pray with and for them. It is good that you work. It is better that you are out of debt or getting out of debt, but it is best that you save and give away as much money as you can, being able to respond quickly and generously to needs as they surface. It is good to come home at night. It is better that you spend time with your family and not watch so much television. It is best that you talk and speak words of life to each other. Obviously there is nothing wrong with edifying recreation. We all need rest, but this is very different from stultifying prodigality that marks most of us. *And finally, if you are to walk carefully in this troubled world, then you need to live Christ-centered lives.* You need to be clear on God's big picture. He makes it clear in Ephesians 1:4, 5, 7, 10 and many other places. He delights in the salvation of His people to the praise of the glory of His grace. Everything that happens in the world is to bring this to fruition. So begin to see the tsunamis, the Presidential elections, our economic woes, and your own trials as part of the big picture of sanctifying God's people and saving all His elect. And then give yourself to this noble work, heeding Paul's command to give your bodies as living sacrifices to God. Spend and be spent for the gospel. Allow yourself to be poured out as a drink offering for Jesus. You can rest when you get to heaven. You can retire then. If you have good health, stay at kingdom building until God takes your health or your life. Look to the day when you hear Jesus say, "Well done, good and faithful servant. Enter into the joy of eternal rest."

Don't Blink

*I urge you therefore, brethren, to present your bodies
a living and holy sacrifice.*

ROMANS 12:1

FRIEDRICH SCHLEIERMACHER SAID IN his *On Religion: Speeches to Its Cultured Despisers,*[57] that due to the intellect of those in the Enlightenment it was necessary to distance oneself from the old theology, that we could not expect enlightened man to believe it. He said that if we want to reach these cultured despisers of the gospel, then we must abandon such teachings as the deity of Christ, His virgin birth, and His resurrection. Liberal Protestants bought into this in the nineteenth and twentieth centuries, resulting in the emptying of their churches. Why did liberals take this position? They believed the Christian faith was losing ground in the west, and in order to reach the well educated it was necessary and proper to give way on orthodox theology. George Marsden in *Reforming Fundamentalism*[58] makes a similar observation with the Christian fundamentalists after the Scopes trial of 1925. By the late 1940s fundamentalists who distanced themselves from anti-intellectual, legalistic, and separatist Christians wanted desperately a "place at the table" of theological ideas. The result was the founding of Fuller Seminary and *Christianity Today* magazine. The latter intentionally held to evangelical theology, but leaned to the left on political and social issues. Marsden documents the sad decline of Fuller Seminary from solid evangelicalism to something far different today, a denial of biblical inerrancy.

Could it be that the seeker-friendly movement of Willow Creek and others following in her wake have yielded to the Sirenian song of respectability by combining consumerism, entertainment, and the homo-

---

57. Schleiermacher, *On Religion: Speeches to Its Cultured Despisers,* 84.
58. Marsden, *Reforming Fundamentalism,* 153ff.

geneous concept (churches grow best when people of the same color and socio-economic status worship together)? No doubt their desire to reach people for Christ is authentic, just as Schleiermacher's was. They say they are committed to theological orthodoxy but they seem to be decidedly non-theological, driven by the business principle that the consumer is sovereign. Thus they say that we must give him what he wants, not necessarily what he needs. The old Protestant position is to have a theologically driven ministry, one that gets as far as possible from the ancient heresy of Pelagianism, a belief that man does not have original sin, that he chooses to become a sinner. The theologically driven ministry takes its cue from Biblical doctrines such as God's sovereignty, unconditional election, total depravity, particular redemption, calling men to holiness as they submit to a holy God who redeems only through the blood of Christ, who calls all men everywhere to repent because God has fixed a day in which He will judge the world. This older view is quite aware of the impossibility of ministry, thus casting itself on the sufficiency of Christ, the sovereignty of God, and the ministry of the Holy Spirit.

David Wells in his book *Above All Earthly Pow'rs*,[59] mentions *The Churching Of America, 1776–1990* where the authors say that what has historically caused churches to grow is a deep commitment to doctrine and a distinctiveness from the culture. The liberal church did not embrace this notion of deep commitment and doctrinal orthodoxy and lost members by the millions. The evangelical church of the 1950s to the 1970s did embrace it and consequently grew rapidly. Unfortunately it seems that the seeker friendly movement no longer believes that deep commitment, sacrifice, the hard sayings of Jesus, and theology are what people want. Wells predicts that the seeker friendly churches will begin losing members because the people are not being challenged, that entertainment grows old after a while.

It appears to me that some of these seeker friendly churches are already realizing this and seeking to make changes. I have read books by Brian MacLaren,[60] and Donald Miller[61] who say that the eighteen to thirty-five year olds today do not like the seeker friendly approach to doing church, that what they want is authenticity. However these people still

59. Wells, *Above All Earthly Pow'rs: Christ in a Postmodern World*, 257.

60. McLaren, *The Church on the Other Side: Doing Ministry in the Postmodern Matrix*, 36.

61. Miller, *Blue Like Jazz: Nonreligious Thoughts on Christian Spirituality*, 177ff.

do not like dogma. Thus we need to go light on doctrine. Why? That is because the post modern mind does not believe in absolute truth. Some of these writers, for example, want to make a false dichotomy between God's incomprehensibility and His knowability. The argument goes like this—since there are many things about God we do not or cannot know, then how can we be so sure about other doctrines Christians have heretofore been sure about? They have in mind things like homosexuality, one way to God, and the doctrine of eternal punishment.

I suggest that seeker friendly churches and emerging churches will follow liberal Protestants and begin to decline as well. The biblical fact is that God calls us to be living sacrifices and the wonderful thing is that He blesses such sacrifice. Sacrifice to Christ is a mark of a revival life. The truly converted rise to the challenge and live with zeal and passion.

So, if you are a member of a theologically driven church or if you as a pastor are committed to such ministry, then don't blink. Stay at it! I know other churches have bling, big programs, lots of excitement, but it will not last. What are you to do? Stay the course. Believe your theology. Seek God. Realize that if the Holy Spirit does not come upon your ministry then nothing of significance will happen. Acknowledge your helplessness but at the same time be hopeful. God is glorified in the salvation of sinners, and we are to keep on preaching because He has many people in this city.

Proof of Ownership

These are the heads of their father's households.

EXODUS 6:14

E XODUS 6:14–27 MAY, AT first glance, seem totally irrelevant to us who are living the fast-paced life of modernity. After all it is merely a genealogy. What does this have to do with us, you may ask?

Just prior to Thomas Hooker immigrating to the new world in the 1630's and founding the city of Hartford, he served as a minister of a small church in rural England. A woman in his church, the wife of Sir Francis Drake, was convinced she had committed the unpardonable sin, and was thus condemned to hell. Hooker helped her work her way through her despondency, convincing her to rest on the testimony of Scripture for her eternal salvation.[62]

Doubt by Christians is a common occurrence. How, you may ask, can we be sure we are believers? How can we be sure that what we believe about God, Christ, man, and eternal life is true? After all so many religions vie for our affections?

The genealogy in Exodus 6 seems to be completely out of context. Why, in the midst of a vital narrative about Israel's release from Egyptian bondage, do we find it? A close look at the genealogy reveals that Moses is following precisely earlier and later genealogies, and that he stops going through all the sons of Israel at the third one mentioned—Levi. From there he mentions in more detail the various sons of Levi, even mentioning later major players in God's unfolding plan of redemption—men like Nadab, Abihu, Korah, and Phinehas. The key to the genealogy, however, is seen in verses 26–27 when we are told that Moses and Aaron are the same ones to whom the Lord said, "Bring out the sons of Israel from the land of Egypt according to their hosts." It was most probable that people were

---

62. Bush, Jr., *The Writings of Thomas Hooker: Spiritual Adventure in Two Worlds*, 4.

not ready to accept Moses' testimony that he was Yahweh's chosen instrument of deliverance. The people needed more testimony, and to where did Moses look for it? He went to the Scriptures. He looked to the revelation of God's word for proof that he follows directly in the line of Jacob, as do the others mentioned in the text. Thus Moses has divine authority for his call, found in the testimony of God's word.

Maybe you doubt God's call to eternal salvation. Some do so because of an overly tender conscience. They seem to dwell more on their sin than the goodness and mercy of God. Some have such a sinful past that they doubt God could really forgive them. Some battle to a significant degree present and recurring sin, or perhaps recent heinous sin. They are often listening to the accusations of the devil, and thus lack any peace or assurance that they are God's. Some have imbibed of false teaching, being convinced that works and faith merit our salvation. Others have such a truncated view of the eternal decree of election that they believe they are not elect, therefore being incapable of salvation, no matter what they do. Some believe they have committed the unpardonable sin. And others experience what the Puritans called the "dark night of the soul," times where they feel as though God has deserted them, that their prayers get no farther than the ceiling. It seems to me that all Christians have experienced this dark night at some time or another.

How do we gain a greater assurance of our eternal salvation? Well, it does not come by baptism, whether as an infant or an adult. While important, one's baptism is no guarantee of eternal salvation. The same can be said for a decision one has made for Christ. Just because you walked forward, raised your hand, or joined a church is no guarantee of saving faith. Finally the fact that you had an emotional encounter with God is no guarantee of heaven either. Many have had such and give no indication of saving faith. How then can you know for certain your eternal standing with God? It comes, dear friend, just as Moses showed in the genealogy, by the testimony of Scripture. Is their evidence of repentance and faith? (See John 1:12, 6:47, Romans 10:9–10). Is there evidence of a changed life? (See 1 John 2:3ff, 3:23ff, 4:2ff, 5:1ff, 5:13). I did not ask if you are perfect. I know you are not, but has your life changed, becoming progressively more conformed to the image of Christ? And finally there is what the theologians call *testimonium spiritu sancti internum,* the internal witness of the Holy

Spirit,[63] (see Romans 8:14–16). Has the Holy Spirit ever impressed upon you that you are a child of God? God wants you to know the glory of your union with Christ, the marvelous hope of sins forgiven, and the gift of eternal life. Appeal to the Bible. Base your life on what it says.

63. Reymond, *A New Systematic Theology of the Christian Faith*, 81.

A Sober Warning

Be imitators of God . . . walk in love.

EPHESIANS 5:1

BETWEEN THIRTY-FIVE AND FORTY-THREE percent of Americans claim to be born again while those whom pollster George Barna calls "evangelical" comprise seven or eight percent of the U.S. population. In 2001 thirty-three percent of born again Christians have been divorced, compared with thirty-four percent of the rest of our population. Even more of a concern is the statistic that states that ninety percent of all born again folk divorced after they accepted Christ. And the divorce rate in 1999 among evangelicals was exactly that of the general population—twenty-five percent.[64] Born again people have virtually the same levels of divorce, adultery, fornication, and use of pornography as the rest of the population. Evangelicals are those who believe in the Trinity, the sinfulness of man, the reality of heaven and hell, the need to receive Christ as one's Lord and Savior, and the obligation to speak to others about their souls. Of the eight percent of Americans who are evangelical, sixteen per cent admit to swearing, using profanity in public; while twelve percent admit to regular use of pornography. In other words, professing Christians look far too much like the world in which we live. Is there little wonder that so many are not interested in the Christian faith? Is there little wonder why the western church is mired in worldliness, seeing so few conversions, facing the onslaught of militant Islam that threatens our very existence? Should we be surprised at the anemia so present in our churches? What good is the Christian faith doing for those who profess it?

It is with this in view that we would do well to heed the sober warning from Ephesians 5:1–6. First we find that Paul has issued two positive com-

---

64. Sider, *The Scandal of the Evangelical Conscience: Why Are Christians Living Just Like the Rest of the World?* 18.

mands in verses 1–2, commanding that we always mimic (a transliteration of the Greek word used here) God. Peter tells us to do the same thing in 1 Peter 1:15–16, to be holy as God is holy. And Jesus drives home the need to love one another and thus fulfill His new commandment, (John 13:34). The foundation for such holy living is Christ's love for us, knowing that He gave Himself up for us, an offering and sacrifice to God. This is Old Testament language concerning the animal sacrifices which went up to God as a fragrant aroma. But Paul also gives a series of negative commands, verses 3–4, saying that immorality (the Greek word from which we get pornography) or any impurity or greed is not even to be mentioned among believers. In other words these sorts of things ought never to be done by God's people. These negative commands do not only address sinful acts, but they also appeal to our hearts, minds, and souls. We are also continually to put away the slightest hint of obscenity or profanity. Such words ought never to be uttered by those who so regularly sing the praises of the God of Zion. Then the silly talk, literally "moronic words", (one thinks today of the preponderance of unnecessary emails sent daily) and coarse jesting are to be eschewed. The word for coarse jesting very early had the connotation of wittiness, but quickly evolved to mean sexual innuendo and double entendre. Dirty and crude jokes, lascivious emails, making fun of one's appearance or body are totally inconsistent with those who claim to know Christ. Instead the practice of thanksgiving in one's speech is to characterize those bought by the blood of Christ.

And in verses five and six Paul gives a grave reason for these commands, warning that no immoral (the Greek word is *porneia*) or impure person or covetous man, who is an idolater, has an inheritance in the kingdom of God. In other words, regardless of one's profession of faith, his conversion experience, or his good works and money he gives away, if his life is characterized by ungodly living then he has no reason to think that he is in Christ, and will go to heaven when he dies. Al, are you telling us that you no longer believe "once saved, always saved"? No, I am not saying that, but the Scripture is plain here and so many other places, (Matthew 7:22–23, 1 Corinthians 6:9, Hebrews 10:26–27). There is a complementarity of truth. God gives eternal salvation, but those professing Christians who live in disobedience will be judged eternally. One's profession of faith, if given life by the regenerating work of the Holy Spirit, will result in a new way of living. A new heart yields new speech, new values, new actions. Can a true Christian fall into immorality, impurity, greed, filthiness, silly talk, and coarse jesting? Yes but he is different than the church going hypocrite or admitted unbeliever. He will tremble at God's word, (Isaiah 66:1–2). He will eventually see his sin and feel deeply convicted and burdened by it, even sickened by it, and will repent, running to Christ and His shed blood for refuge. He will make progress in holiness. He will not continue to excuse his sinful actions, speech, and values. He will own up to them and repent of them, making progress in gospel holiness. To put it more simply, based on the text mentioned above, the true Christian will find his life motivated and controlled by the love of Christ, a love that is not selfish but sacrificial, not niggardly but extravagant. He will be awed and overwhelmed by Christ's love made manifest in His temptation in the Garden of Gethsemane, and His willingness to suffer untold horror at Calvary on his behalf. He will come to understand that impurity and holiness are oxymoronic. He will come to glory in the language of the redeemed, (see Romans 12:9–13).

Here's the sober warning—even professing Christians whose lives are marked by immorality, impurity, covetousness, profanity, foolish talk, and sexual innuendo are in serious trouble. If this is true of you, then I ask that you soberly, seriously, humbly ask yourself, "Do I have good reason to believe that I am in Christ? Do my lifestyle, speech, actions, and values resemble those who have hearts changed by the work of the Holy Spirit?" Do not be deceived by false religious talk, when preachers say, "Peace, Peace," for if these mark your life, then there is no peace, (Ezekiel 13:10). Paul says in Romans 6:22 that because we have been set free from sin and become enslaved to righteousness we derive our benefit, resulting in sanctification and the outcome of eternal life. Regeneration leads to sanctification, loving what God loves and hating what God hates. The ungodly, on the other hand, gain hell. Paul declares in Romans 2:5–6 that the goodness of God is to lead you to repentance, but because of stubbornness and an unrepentant heart you may be storing up wrath for yourself in the day of wrath and revelation of the righteous judgment of God who will render to every man according to his deeds.

In other words, truth faith is transforming, and it is always motivated by the grace of God bestowed on those for whom Christ died. If you are reading this and not the least bit concerned for your soul, then it is likely that you are not in Christ at all; but if you are troubled by this, if you wrestle with these sins, if you see them for what they are (rebellion against God), if you tremble at God's word, if these words slay you, devastate you, then likely you are in Christ. You will always battle sin in this life (see

Romans 7:23ff), but the true believer makes progress with his sin over the years. So, heed the sober warning, come back to Christ or come to Him for the first time, asking the Holy Spirit to convict you daily of your sin, to work sanctification in you, to give you a tender heart that hates what God hates and loves what God loves.

Celebrating the Indicatives, Ignoring the Imperatives

If then you have been raised up with Christ, keep seeking the things above,
where Christ is, seated at the right hand of God.

COLOSSIANS 3:1

HERMAN RIDDERBOS IN HIS classic theological work on Pauline theology, *Paul: An Outline of His Theology*, goes to great length to describe Paul's use of the Greek indicative and imperative moods.[65] He says, "It is evident that this new life is not to be understood as a transcendent stream of life that pours into man from the outside, and that develops in him naturally whereby there would no longer be any place for human responsibility and decision . . . ." Ridderbos is pointing out that Paul uses the indicative mood to declare certain glorious truths about all who are united to Christ in His death and resurrection. Paul, for example, uses the indicative mood almost exclusively in Romans 1–11 where he lays down marvelous truths about what God has done for us, given us in Christ. The indicative, however, always yields the imperative, the mood of command. Thus in Romans 12:1ff Paul, after laying down the indicatives, moves to the imperatives, calling us to obedience.

Certainly we ought to celebrate the marvelous indicatives of the Christian life. How, for example, can we not exult in all Paul declares in Ephesians 1:3–14, saying that we have every spiritual blessing in Christ, that God has chosen us, predestined us, adopted us, redeemed us, sealed us, etc. How can we not glory in the fact that we have died with Christ, been buried with Him, and raised with Him to newness of life (Romans 6:1ff).

But Pauline theology never stops at the indicative, for the gospel declarations of our union with Christ always give way to the imperatives. In Romans 6:12 Paul says, "Therefore do not let sin reign in your mortal body that you should obey its lusts." In Romans 12:2 Paul says, "And do

---

65. Ridderbos, *Paul: An Outline of His Theology*, 253ff.

not be conformed to this world, but be transformed by the renewing of your mind." God calls us, as His blood bought people, to live in the biblical tension of grace and law. Scripture teaches three uses of the Law of God. First, it is a school master or tutor to drive the sinner to Christ, showing him his sin and judgment, and need of a Savior, (Galatians 3:24). Second, the law has a civil use. People, families, and nations who honor authority, refrain from murder, adultery, stealing, false witness, and coveting will generally live peaceable, long lives on earth, (Ephesians 6:2–3). Most Christians today agree with these first two uses of the Law of God, but there is a third use that Reformed believers have long embraced. This one is the practical use of the Law. The believer is to use the Law of God as a guide to holiness. He is to evaluate his life and practice in light of God's imperatives, and where he is failing, is to repent, asking the Holy Spirit for grace to obey. Steve Brown put it this way in *A Scandalous Freedom*, "The Law is to keep believers at the foot of the cross."[66] By this he means the Law shows us our sin, and draws us back to the cross for repentance.

Richard Owen Roberts, an expert on and strong proponent of revival, says that we need to learn the difference between "ego repentance and evangelical repentance".[67] The former means I may say I am sorry, even ask God to forgive me because I was caught, or I simply want relief from the one against whom I sinned. Evangelical repentance means that we realize our sin primarily is against God, and this means a change of mind and heart that yields a change of behavior. We tend to take far too lightly our sin, meaning that we quickly return to it, like a dog to its vomit.

Could it be that we are celebrating the indicatives but ignoring the imperatives? Colossians 3:1 reminds us of the glorious truth that we have been raised up with Christ. This truth, however, means that we are continually to keep seeking the things above, where Christ is. Paul tells Timothy to discipline (our word for gymnasium) himself for the purpose of godliness. The idea is one of self-denial, self-control, subduing the deeds of the flesh, putting off the old man and putting on the new man, of putting to death the deeds of the body, of perfecting holiness in the fear of God.

Celebrating the indicatives can lead to ignoring the imperatives, hindering holiness in God's people, thus grieving the Holy Spirit, thus mitigating the progress of the gospel in a family, church, or community. I

66. Brown, *A Scandalous Freedom: The Radical Nature of the Gospel*, 231.
67. Roberts, *Repentance; The First Word of the Gospel*, 115.

wonder, for example, if pastors ought to consider whether or not the public consumption of alcoholic beverages, especially in church sponsored meetings, is quenching the very Holy Spirit whom they know they need to grant power in ministry. I wonder if pastors ought to rethink the possible temptation to church members by citing movies or television programs in their sermons with lewd speech and behavior. I wonder if pastors have really considered what they are doing when they use crass or profane language from the pulpit on in email correspondence in order to *connect* with our post modern world. Are these things pleasing to the Lord? Is the Holy Spirit smiling upon such things?

Surely self-righteousness and legalism are harmful, and we have all been guilty of these in one way or another. Not too many years ago pastors were very private about their sin, and perhaps went too far in concealing it, giving a false impression of holiness to their people. And surely pastors ought to let their people know they struggle with sin too. But in our desire to express vulnerability shouldn't we also be seeking to subdue the deeds of the flesh? Our freedom in Christ is never a license to sin or to celebrate our failures. But the current practice of some pastors to celebrate the indicatives while ignoring the imperatives to walk in a manner worthy of our calling, of being holy as God is holy, of putting to death the deeds of the body is equally as dangerous. This practice is harmful to the cause of Christ and His gospel that we love and are called to proclaim.

Apostasy

And Judas Iscariot, who was one of the twelve, went off to the chief priests,
in order to betray Him to them.

MARK 14:10

How could Judas do it? How could he betray his friend, the One who called him to be an apostle, the One whom he had served for three years? To be sure others in Scripture had been betrayed—Demas left Paul for this present world. Many left Jesus in John 6:66 after His strong message, refusing to follow Him any longer. But this is so much worse. Consider the marvelous privileges Judas had. He has seen Jesus heal lepers, cast out demons, raise people from the dead, walk on water, feed the five thousand, calm a storm, preach profound sermons. He also seemed to have impeccable integrity. After all, he was given responsibility to handle the disciples' money. You don't appoint Treasurer of your church or business one even remotely suspect in character. We are told later that Judas pilfered the money box, but no one knew it at the time. So, how could this happen? To be sure, Jesus refers to Judas in His prayer of John 17 as the son of perdition, and in Mark 14:49 Jesus told the mob who apprehended Him that this was in fulfillment of prophecy, meaning Judas was foreordained for this gruesome deed. Nonetheless, he was responsible for his actions. Again we have the complementarity of truth. God ordains yet Judas is completely responsible. We cannot understand these things simply in the mind. They don't make sense. They can only fit in the heart. He was not a robot. He made the decision to betray Jesus.

Be sure of this sober truth—you have the seeds of apostasy in your soul. Therefore you are to be vigilant, knowing that your adversary the devil is like a roaring lion, roaming about, seeking to devour whomever he may. How are you to stand against apostasy, leaving the faith? After all, isn't betrayal the very essence of apostasy? Consider this—if you are trusting in anything but Jesus to keep from it, then you may well fail.

You have marvelous Christian privileges. If you live in the U.S. then you have religious freedom, a plethora of Bible translations, a vast array of Christian books and periodicals, Christian music of every stripe. That's good, but these won't keep you from apostasy. Perhaps you attend a Bible preaching church, one committed to the inerrancy of Scripture. That's good, but this won't keep you from apostasy. Maybe you have Christian parents who prayed with and for you, who lived out and instructed you in Christian living. That's good too, but these won't keep you from apostasy. Maybe you have warm feelings of love for Jesus. That's good, but it will not keep you from apostasy. Maybe you had a dramatic conversion that you constantly review with awe and wonder. That's good, but it will not keep you from apostasy. Perhaps you have a great deal of knowledge about the Trinity, the two natures of Christ, the ministry of the Holy Spirit. Perhaps you have a deep knowledge of the Bible and love to teach it, receiving warm accolades from those who listen to you. That's good, but these will not keep you from apostasy. And perhaps you have been used mightily by God in the past, in the conversion and growth in grace of many. That's good, but these deeds will not keep you from apostasy.

Apostasy is a very serious matter. It will make shipwreck of your faith, strip you of joy and power in the Holy Spirit, and if continued, will send you to hell. "Anyone who lays aside the Law of Moses dies without mercy on the testimony of two or three witnesses. How much severer punishment do you think he will deserve who has trampled under foot the Son of God, who has regarded as unclean the blood of the covenant by which he was sanctified, and has insulted the Spirit of grace . . . it is a terrifying thing to fall into the hands of the living God" (Hebrews 10:28–31). Why is this so serious? Because it is exactly the same thing Judas did, betraying the One who showed such mercy and grace, causing the Son to be crucified again, putting Him to open shame. Such a one cannot be renewed again to repentance, (Hebrews 6:6).

Wait a second, Al. What about eternal security? What about "once saved, always saved?" I know. What a wonderful doctrine and I wholly subscribe to it. But what do we do with Hebrews 10:28ff? What about the seven letters in Revelation 2–3 where time after time Jesus says, "To Him who overcomes, I will grant Him to eat from the tree of life in the Paradise of God . . . He who overcomes will thus be clothed in white garments, and I will not erase his name from the book of life, and I will confess his name before My Father and His angels?"

Watch over your heart with all diligence for from it flows the springs of life, (Proverbs 4:23). How do you do that? You must be faithful in heart work. By this I mean go straight to your heart, not your actions, not your speech, not your feelings. Consider the beatitudes. Do you realize how desperate you are for grace? You are bankrupt without Jesus. You are out of options. You have no hope. Even as a believer, if you entertain the notion that you have now arrived and can make it today without Jesus, then you are in big trouble. You are to grieve, to mourn over your sin. Let it break your heart, even the "little things." Be willing to accept rebuke from a spouse or brother or sister in Christ. That's meekness. And then realize that because you are so vile in your flesh, you must hunger and thirst for righteousness, for the living Christ, not unlike a man who has not had water for two days. He thinks only of water.

Then cut back the root sins as far as you can. You cannot uproot them in this life, but you can cut them back to ground level, so to speak, as you do in pruning a bush. I suggest your root sins are pride (I don't have to listen to God), unbelief (I won't trust what God says), and rebellion (I know what God says, and I believe it, but I refuse to do it). These may lead to sexual sin and broken relationships through pride; to bitterness, anger, resentment, or despair through unbelief; and a failure to submit to authority and all the consequent problems through rebellion.

Finally, if you are to guard yourself against apostasy you must kiss the Son. "Do homage, kiss the Son, lest He become angry and you perish in the way," (Psalm 2:12). Consider the immoral woman of Luke 7:36ff, who knelt at the feet of Jesus, kissing His dirty feet, bathing them with her hair in her tears. You may think, "How quaint!" But don't miss the point of the story. You are that immoral woman. Before a holy God, even the best, the most moral of you, were condemned to hell because of willful rebellion. But God has had mercy. Dwell on this daily, live in this truth, and see God move your heart to profound devotion to Jesus, keeping you from apostasy.

Extremism

With all humility and gentleness, with patience,
showing forbearance to one another in love.

EPHESIANS 4:2

ALL WHO KNEW HIM said that Roger Williams was a godly man, well versed in the Reformed faith, a winsome man with profound spiritual gifts. However he ran into trouble very quickly after his arrival in the Massachusetts Bay Colony in 1631. He refused the offer to be the pastor of the Congregational Church in Boston, because it was associated with the Church of England, a church which he considered apostate. He also refused the pastoral position at the church in Salem (a congregation comprised of Pilgrims who were separatists). Though the people also believed the Church of England to be apostate and had formerly separated from it, they nonetheless worshipped at such congregations when back in England. Williams could not fellowship with people given to such hypocrisy. He also believed the church had been under control of Antichrist since 400 A.D. Thus any possibility of a true, apostolic church was long lost. This meant he questioned the validity of any church, any pastor or church leadership to baptize or admit members. And since the church was in such disrepair, and hopelessly so, it really was a waste of time to evangelize the Indians in New England. Why, he thought, bring converts into such a corrupt church?[68]

The views of Roger Williams were too much for the magistrate at Massachusetts Bay and they eventually banished him to Rhode Island. Roger Williams is the father of our form of government, the separation between church and state, the idea that the civil magistrate has no authority over the life of the church. This was a departure from the accepted Erastian view of England and Europe at the time, where the church was

---

68. Gaustad, *Liberty of Conscience: Roger Williams in America*, 83.

118

seen as subservient to the state. So Roger Williams did a lot of good things, but his extremism was harmful and his legacy, therefore, tainted.

Why can't we keep the car on the road? Why must we persist in damaging our witness to the world by extreme behavior and theology? What kind of message are we sending to the world when our marriages so easily end in divorce, when fathers are overbearing and manipulative with their children, when husbands lord their authority over their wives, when wives cannot stay at home, spending money on frivolous things? Why do we have so many Christian denominations? Why are there so many Reformed denominations? Why are there so many church splits? Why are there Christian people we avoid in the supermarket? Why the splintering of so many relationships?

I suggest the problem is deeply rooted in our hearts. We, by nature, are prone to extremism, and the root of it is the idol of control, our own agenda. We are so enamored with our understanding of an issue, so intent on making our agenda everyone else's agenda, that we do not seriously consider what we are doing. An idol is anything, even a good or true thing that takes the place of God in our hearts. When this happens it will sooner or later come out in our speech and actions. I suggest the root sin here is pride. We simply think we know best, that we have a better understanding of the issue than anyone else.

Are you an extremist? Are you pushing your agenda on other people—your spouse, your children, your employees, your church? This is a very subtle thing. You may have the big picture in view, knowing what needs to happen in a particular situation. However your desire to have it your way may subvert the very good you seek to achieve. For example, you know the doctrine of God's sovereignty is true and immensely practical, and you long for your friends or church members to grasp it and apply it. However you undermine it by running rough shod over any who question it. You know you are to love your wife sacrificially, but your insistence that she follow your lead may meet with resistance. Perhaps you have not established in her mind and heart a sincere desire to love her as Christ loved the church and gave Himself up for her. And you know this new product line will be good for your company, but in your excitement you fail to bring others along with you in your thought process. You are so far in front of them that they cannot see you in order to follow you. These result in bitter division and strife.

What is the solution to extremism? Paul, in Ephesians 4:1ff begins the practical section of his epistle by laying down the doctrine of the church, building on the foundation of chapters 1–3 where he has told us of our identity in Christ, of how Christ by His blood has broken down the middle wall of partition between Jew and Gentile, praying that we would know the height and depth and breadth and length of the love of Christ, believing that God is able to do exceeding abundantly beyond all that we ask or think, according to the power that works within us. From there he exhorts us to walk in a manner worthy of our calling in Christ Jesus. And how are we to do that? He begins by exhorting us to display forbearance, long-suffering toward one another. How are we to do that? It comes by practicing humility and gentleness. In Philippians 2:3–4 Paul puts it another way. We are to do nothing from selfishness or empty conceit. Rather we are to consider other people as more important than ourselves; and the means by which we accomplish this is our union with the Christ who emptied Himself for us, taking the form of a bond servant.

Here's what we are doing when we give ourselves to extremism. In essence we are saying, "My idol of control, and the pride which under girds it, alone is able to bring me comfort, peace, and notoriety. I put my trust in control." Consider, however, this *argumentum ad absurdum*, based on Colossians 1:16ff, substituting our idol for Christ. "All things were created through my control, and my control is before all things, and in my control all things hold together. My control is the head of the body of Christ, and my control is the beginning, the firstborn from the dead, so that my control may come to have first place in everything. For it was the Father's good pleasure for all the fullness to dwell in my control, and through my control to reconcile all things to God, having made peace through my control, through my control, I say, whether things on earth or things in heaven."

Isn't that what you are doing when you must have it your way? Aren't you guilty of putting yourself, your idol, in place of Christ? What must you do? You need to repent and believe the gospel of grace every day. You are repenting when you see just how serious and pervasive this is. You are believing when you come again to Jesus, seeking His forgiveness and power to live out who you really are. Come back to Jesus now.

The Church Triumphant

. . . from whom every family in heaven and on earth derives its name.

Ephesians 3:15

David Brainerd the great missionary to the American Indians was born in April 1718 at Haddam, CT. His father, a legislator in Connecticut, died when David was nine years old, and his mother died when he was fourteen. He lived with a godly aunt and uncle until he was eighteen, and then tried farming for a year at nearby Durham, CT. Though growing up in the local Congregational Church, Brainerd was soundly converted at age nineteen, and then studied at nearby Yale College. He left after a few months with a recurring illness, returning one year later at the height of the evangelical revival at Yale under the preaching ministry of George Whitefield. Brainerd, in his intemperate zeal, spoke in wonder at the Rector of Yale College not falling down dead for fining students for their evangelical zeal. When Brainerd also suggested that a tutor had no more grace than a chair, he was expelled from Yale, thus never completing his degree. The state of Connecticut required all ministers to graduate from Yale, Harvard, or a European university, and Brainerd was thus denied ordination. He answered the call to become a missionary to American Indians. Brainerd's life was fraught with recurring illness, loneliness, and depression. If Jonathan Edwards was able to overcome his melancholy through walks in the woods, looking at the beauty of nature, this seemed not to work for Brainerd. In fact nothing worked to remove his depression. Thankfully it did not result in suicidal thoughts, as these did with the great hymn writer William Cowper, but they nonetheless were a terrible burden to him. After serving the Housatonic Indians near Stockbridge, Massachusetts and several tribes at the forks of the Delaware River where hundreds were converted in a very brief time, and finally after a year or so near Lebanon, CT with the Iroquois Indians, Brainerd began losing his battle with tuberculosis. He made his way to the home of Jonathan and

Sarah Edwards in May 1747 and died at their home several months later.[69] He was cared for by Edwards' eighteen year old daughter Jerusha with whom Brainerd has been romantically linked.[70] Brainerd died at the age of twenty-nine, being a Christian for only eight years and a missionary for only four years. No one has more impacted the modern missionary movement than David Brainerd. Why and how did he live with such usefulness to God in the midst of his terrible circumstances?

He understood what Paul said in the verse mentioned above, that he was part of the church of God from whom every family in heaven and earth derives its name. Paul cannot be referring to every family in the world, whether Christian or non-Christian. That's because the content of Paul's prayer refers to being strengthened with power through the Holy Spirit in the inner person . . . that they may be rooted in love . . . that they may know the love of Christ which surpasses all understanding. So, those mentioned as "every family in heaven and earth," are the church on earth and in heaven, what theologians call the "church militant and the church triumphant."

So what was it that sustained David Brainerd and so many others in the midst of harsh circumstances? What can help you in the temptations and tribulations you face? How can you live a more consistent revival life? It is the knowledge and practical application that your union with Christ empowers you to overcome any temptation or tribulation which the world throws at you. Consider this, dear Christian. You are a member of the church militant. I don't mean you are to be caustic, harsh, or in an attack mode toward those outside the church. By militant I mean you are part of the church now on earth which is called by Paul to fight the good fight of faith, to lay hold of the eternal life to which you have been called. You are to realize that your struggle is not against flesh and blood, but against rulers, against authorities, against world forces of darkness, against spiritual forces of wickedness in high places. You are to rejoice in the indicatives of God's grace and love, and you are to obey, to live out the imperatives to perfect holiness in the fear of God.

To go further, however, you are part of the church now in heaven, the church triumphant. The writer to the Hebrews tells us that we do not go to a mountain that may be touched and to a blazing fire . . . but to Mount

69. Piper, *The Hidden Smile of God*, 123ff.

70. I believe there was something to this due to older sister Esther Edwards Burr's diary where she mentions their affection for each other. *Esther Burr's Journal*, 29.

Zion, the city of the living God . . . to the general assembly and the church of the first born which are enrolled in heaven . . . and to Jesus the mediator of a new covenant, (Hebrews 12:18–24). John tells us that he looked and saw a great multitude that no one could count, from every nation and all the tribes and peoples and tongues, standing before the throne and before the Lamb, clothed in white robes and palm branches were in their hands; and they cry out with a loud voice, saying, "Salvation to our God who sits on the throne, and to the Lamb." In other words, the very fact that you are part of the family of God now on earth (the church militant), and one day in heaven (the church triumphant) means that God promises you the power and authority to overcome any temptation or trial that comes at you. In 1 Corinthians 10:1ff Paul is using the negative example of Israel in the wilderness to warn the Corinthians against falling back into idolatry. He says that God gives them what they need to overcome temptation, that with it He will provide a means of escape. To be sure, your privileged position as a child of God does not negate temptation anymore than it did Israel's position, but His union with you gives you what you need to overcome any and all temptation; and the very fact you persevere in them proves your union with Christ. But God also promises to overcome every tribulation that you face. Paul asks in Romans 8:35ff who can separate us from the love of Christ. And the answer is nothing and no one. The trials, tribulations, and hardships you face do not separate the child of God from His love. In fact this love enables you to overcome them.

So, practically how do you live as a member of the church militant, looking to that day when you will be part of the church triumphant? You must abide or continue in Christ, (see John 15:1–7). More specifically, each day you must continue in God's love for you. Never allow yourself, dear Christian, to doubt or deny God's love for you. Continue in the electing, foreknowing, redeeming, and interceding love of God in Christ. You must also abide in the word of God. I mean here the written word of God through daily reading and meditation on Holy Scripture, but I also mean continuing in your vital relationship with the living word, the Lord Jesus Christ. Speak to Him. Think on Him. Speak to others about Him. And continue in the visible word, the sacrament of the Lord's Supper. This alone sustains you as you move to Mount Zion and the church triumphant.

Preoccupation with the Temporal

Martha, Martha, you are worried and bothered about so many things.

LUKE 10:41

To BORROW A LINE that pokes fun at my southern heritage and red necks—you may be a workaholic if your home is just another office. You may be a workaholic if you take office equipment with you wherever you go, even on vacations. You may be a workaholic if work makes you happier than anything else in life. You may be a workaholic if you frequently "problem solve" work situations in your mind when on your own time. And you may be a workaholic if you get restless on a vacation (if you even take them) and sometimes cut them short. This is a real problem in our culture, and I am not simply thinking of the physical or emotional implications of being a workaholic. I am more interested in the eternal ones.

The short story reported in Luke 10:38–42 gets at the heart of this matter. There are three players in the story. Mary is sitting at the feet of Jesus, and she is obviously preoccupied with eternal issues that impact temporal ones. She is listening to Jesus expound eternal verities instead of doing more temporal, menial tasks. Martha, on the other hand, is preoccupied with the temporal that could impact the eternal. Instead of learning from the eternal and living Word of God, she has chosen to prepare a meal for Him and those in His party. And Jesus is able to focus on both the eternal and temporal, knowing there are eternal implications to both. Jesus is not Gnostic, thinking that only the spiritual is important. He later prepares breakfast for His disciples on the beach, after His resurrection, as He prepares to restore Peter who has just denied Him. But at this moment He is expounding the words of life and Mary is listening while Martha is not.

I have conducted religious surveys from time to time in our community and one question I ask is, "Why do you think most people here do not attend church or synagogue?" Many people say it's because they don't have the time. I remember reading a magazine article in which John

Kenneth Galbraith was quoted as saying we would one day have a thirty hour work week[71] due to the expected technological advances. As I recall, the report projected the work week would be around thirty hours. Is that your experience, given the internet, email, cell phones, etc.? I didn't think so.

Why this preoccupation with the temporal? I suggest four reasons. One is what many call the "tyranny of the urgent". You know—the squeaky wheel gets the grease. We find this even with Martha. She could reason, "Jesus and His disciples are hungry. Somebody has to feed them. The urgent that seems to need immediate attention is what drives our actions. Two, the temporal is seen and the eternal is unseen. You know what needs to be done at work, at home, in the yard, in your community service project; but making deposits into your eternal bank account is not always so obvious. You have friends who want to play golf on Sunday morning. "Church can wait. My friends need me." Three, the pursuit of the eternal and unseen sometimes seems like being lethargic or lazy, perhaps even being an excuse for negligence. After all, that hour you spend each morning reading your Bible and Christian books while also praying may be used more productively. You could be on the phone working a business deal. Why bother setting Sunday aside for worship and rest. That's another whole day to work your business. And four, success with the temporal tends to deaden our desire for the eternal. The rich fool in Luke 12:15ff is a good example.

Where does this preoccupation take us? First, it brings anxiety here and now. The Greek word for anxiety is literally "a divided mind". If you focus on the temporal then you at one moment may trust God but the very next allow your circumstances to rob you of joy. And second, it brings poverty then and there. Jesus asks, "What does it profit a man to gain the whole world if he forfeits his soul?" What are you to do? Seek first the kingdom of God. Get to the point where you desire supremely the glory of God, the propagation of the gospel, and submission to God's will as it is revealed daily in your life. When you consider the goodness and glory of Jesus, why would you ever be preoccupied with the temporal?

---

71. Beuttler," We Work Too Hard", The author sites John Kenneth Galbraith's *The Affluent Society*, 1958.

Praying with Confidence for Their Conversion

. . . by revelation there was made known to me the mystery.

EPHESIANS 3:3.

PEARL S. BUCK, THE great novelist, who won the Pulitzer Prize in 1932 and the Nobel Prize for literature in 1938, grew up on the mission field in China. Her father was a Presbyterian missionary. In a pamphlet she wrote in 1932, entitled, *Is There a Case for Foreign Missions?* she had this to say,

> Let us face ourselves clearly. Some of us believe in Christ as our fathers did; to some of us he is still the divine son of God, born of the Virgin Mary, conceived by the Holy Spirit. But to many of us he has ceased to be that. Some of us do not know what he is, some of us care less. In the world of our life it does not matter perhaps what he is. If we are asked we will say, 'I admire him of course. He was perhaps the best man who ever lived.' But that is all he is. To you who are young, the sons and daughters of this generation, who must carry on foreign missions after the older ones are gone, it is probable that Christ is no longer a cause . . . Let us face the fact that the old reasons for foreign missions are gone from the minds and hearts of many of us, certainly from those of us who are young.[72]

It appears that Pearl S. Buck did not get it. She did not understand the mystery and the revelation. Paul the Apostle is making a parenthetical statement in Ephesians 3:2-13, seeking to encourage the Ephesian Christians who are disturbed by his imprisonment. Paul wants them to understand why he has been imprisoned. He has been made a steward of God's grace, and that gospel came to him by way of revelation, an unveiling (the Greek word is *apocalupto* from which we get apocalypse) or making clear the gospel once hidden from the Gentiles, but now revealed by the work of the Spirit, (see Romans 16:25-26). Paul speaks in Galatians

72. Buck, *Is There a Case for Foreign Missions?*, 8.

126

2:12ff of receiving this unveiling directly from God. He then refers in this verse to the "mystery" and in verse 4 to "the mystery of Christ". He has two different, though related, things in mind. The *mystery* (something once hidden but now revealed) refers to the gospel of grace being hidden from the Gentiles for thousands of years, being revealed only to the Jews. He mentions this same mystery among the Gentiles in Colossians 1:27. But Paul also refers to the mystery of Christ, a term pregnant with meaning. Among other things, it asks the questions, "Why did Jesus become man? Why must He be sinless? Why did He die? How can a man's death take away my own sin?" This mystery of Christ was made known to Paul (once and for all, an act directed by God specifically to Paul), and he was commissioned by God to proclaim it to the Gentiles, Acts 26:19–20.

Can you see to what great lengths God goes to make known the mystery of Christ? God's great desire is His glory in the salvation of His people from every tongue, tribe, and nation. He will save His people from their sins.

I bring this up because you undoubtedly have friends and family members for whom you have been praying for many years, pleading with God to save them, and nothing seems to be happening. May I suggest that you never, never despair, never give up, never doubt that God will save those whom He has placed on your heart. You may have been praying for many years for a wayward child or lost parent. Don't give up. Believe God will save them. Pray without ceasing, (1 Thessalonians 5:17). Pray until God gives you the answer or until they die.

How can I be so bold as to suggest their salvation? Do I have insight into the mysteries of redemption? Have I been made privy to a brief glance at the Lamb's book of life? Of course not, but consider what Paul is saying about this mystery and revelation in light of the ministry of the Holy Spirit helping you to pray. In Romans 8:26–27 Paul says, "And in the same way the Spirit also helps our weakness; for we do not know how to pray as we should, but the Spirit Himself intercedes for us with groanings too deep for words; and He who searches the hearts knows what the mind of the Spirit is, because He intercedes for the saints according to the will of God." Isn't it true that you pray regularly for certain people to be saved, but for others you tend to drop off in your prayers for them? Why is it that God continues to place these people on your heart? Consider this thought. The Father has chosen a certain people, from eternity past, to be His children; and He sent the Lord Jesus Christ to die for them on Calvary's cross. The Holy Spirit applies that redemption to these people in His time, working through secondary means that include the prayers of God's people. In other words, when the time comes for the Father to apply the work of Christ's redemption by the Spirit upon His elect, the Holy Spirit prompts people to pray for them. God is sovereign in salvation but He works through people, including our prayers. Douglas Kelly, in his book *If God Already Knows, Why Pray?*,[73] puts forth this position, citing southern Presbyterian preachers of the nineteenth century as teaching it.

So what are you to do in this matter of the salvation of your friends and family members? What is your role? You ought to do three things. First, talk to God about people. Plead the promises of God. Sue (like a lawsuit, a formal appeal or request) God for their salvation. Remind Him of His great promises concerning the salvation of the nations. You can begin at Genesis 12:1–3, Psalm 2:8, Psalm 67:4–5, Psalm 96:3, Isaiah 52:10, and 2 Peter 3:9. Second, you must clear the highway of holiness of your own sin. In Isaiah 57:14–15 the prophet says, "Build up, build up, prepare the way, remove every obstacle out of the way of My people. For thus says the high and exalted One who lives forever, whose name is Holy, 'I dwell on a high and holy place, and also with the contrite and lowly of spirit in order to revive the spirit of the lowly and to revive the heart of the contrite.'" How do the root sins of pride, unbelief, and rebellion manifest themselves in this matter of reaching out to the lost in your life? Are you prideful in that you are afraid to speak to friends or family members about their souls? Are you afraid of how they may label you a fanatic, wanting to be accepted by them? Are you given to just plain unbelief, saying, "There is no way my friend, my brother will be saved. He is far too gone. He may even be a reprobate." Or what about rebellion? You know you need to move toward that neighbor who is frankly a nuisance and trouble maker, but you don't like him. And so you maintain your guilty silence.

Finally, talk to people about God. In doing so you don't need necessarily to go through the front door. Check out Moses in Exodus 18, speaking to his pagan father-in-law Jethro, telling him of the mighty things Yahweh had done in the ten plagues, and the parting of the Red Sea. Jethro was so overwhelmed by it that he made sacrifices to Yahweh, referring to Him as the true and living God. For whom are you praying regularly? Perhaps you have been at it for many years, asking God for their conversion. Don't grow weary. Believe they will be saved. Sue God for their salvation. Don't give God rest until He becomes a praise in all the earth.

---

73. Kelly, *If God Already Knows, Why Pray?*

New England Smugness

I praise Thee, Father . . . that Thou didst hide these things from the wise and intelligent and didst reveal them to infants.

MATTHEW 11:25

KATHARINE HEPBURN, THE FOUR time Academy Award winner, was born in Hartford on November 8 1907. Her mother was from the Houghton family of the Corning Glass company, and her father was a physician. Katharine's mother leaned toward Communism, and was very much a liberal politically, socially, and religiously. Kate attended the Kingswood-Oxford Prep School in West Hartford, and had no interest in Christianity. It was simply not an issue in their home. Christopher Andersen, in his biography of Katharine Hepburn, *Young Kate*, says that she was a Connecticut Yankee. "These were people having a fierce pride, who considered themselves more refined than those from other New England states. The Connecticut Yankee views himself as smarter, more enterprising, tougher, more principled, better looking—in short, in every way superior."[74]

John Piper has observed that in the year 1900 ninety percent of the Christians in the world were white, residing in Europe, the United Kingdom, and the United States. One hundred years later, ninety percent of the Christians in the world are non-white, residing in Asia, Africa, and South America. Kenyan scholar John Mbiti has suggested that the center of the church is no longer Geneva, Rome, Athens, Paris, London, or New York but Kinshasa, Buenos Aires, Addis Ababa, and Manila.[75] I rejoice at the profound growth of the gospel in previously pagan and ignorant cultures, further driving home the marvelous promise in Revelation 5, 7, that every tongue, tribe, people, and nation will be represented before the throne of God, giving praise to the glorified Christ in heaven. However,

74. Andersen, *Young Kate*, 117.
75. Jenkins, *The Next Christendom: The Coming of Global Christianity*, 2.

after living in New England for several years I have observed a very troubling trend. I have said many times before, "New England is the trend setter for the rest of the United States. What happens here first, will eventually find its way to the rest of our country." We at Christ Community Presbyterian Church in West Hartford have been, and will continue to labor as diligently and creatively as we can, without compromising the Biblical values of ministry, to reach the lost of Connecticut with the gospel. And while we have had some success among Connecticut Yankees, I must tell you that largely we are not, as of this writing, impacting our culture. The question is, "Why not?"

Read this very carefully and thoughtfully because what has been going on here in Connecticut for well over two hundred years is coming your way, and already is there to some extent. There is a great deal of interest in the gospel among African Americans, Hispanics, Hindus, and Muslims. We have seen a number of people from these groups either make professions of faith in Christ or meet with us in Bible studies to learn more about Christianity. We have a number of relationships with Muslim people, in particular, who are not at all turned off by "religious" talk. The smug, well-educated, sometimes affluent Connecticut Yankee, on the other hand, is generally not at all interested in Christianity, thinking it either below him intellectually or completely irrelevant to his life. He tends to view it as a movement too closely tied with conservative politics. Jesus, in this marvelous chapter on His blessed gospel (Matthew 11), praises His Father that He has hidden the gospel from the wise and intelligent (the Jewish leaders), and revealed it to babes (the humble and contrite, those who are weary and weighed down by their sin and shame). It appears that the Connecticut Yankee and other New Englanders are too smug to see their need for Christ. After leading the way theologically, academically, economically from the time of the Puritan Thomas Hooker who founded Hartford in the 1630's, Connecticut began to embrace the Unitarianism of William Ellery Channing and the liberal theology of Horace Bushnell. She has long prided herself on free thought and free expression. The Connecticut psyche seems hell bent (pardon the pun) on cleansing itself from any vestige of Puritan thought or life. The problems of New England, whether racial, economic, or political seem always to be placed at the feet of the Puritans. They are blamed for everything.

So, what does this mean for us at Christ Community Presbyterian Church in West Hartford, and what does it mean for you in your community and church? I wonder if we ought to take seriously the method of the Apostle Paul. Paul, a Jew with a pedigree, because he loved his people and because the gospel came first to the Jews, went to them first whenever he came to a new town. Mostly, however, they rejected his message, beating him and running him out of town. Before leaving, however, Paul would go to the despised, uncultured, debauched, heathen Gentiles. They heard him gladly. I love my European culture and heritage, and I am perhaps better equipped to minister the gospel to people who are like me; but if they will not listen, then should I not go to those who will listen? Isn't that what God seems to be doing in the world anyway? God resists the proud, but gives grace to the humble. Isaiah said that God looks to those who are humble and contrite, who tremble at His word. One of the staggering principles found throughout Scripture is that God moves toward those who move toward Him. Yes, I know man will not seek God on his own (Romans 3:10ff), but Scripture also says, "Draw near to Me, and I will draw near to you . . . I will permit those who seek Me to find Me," (James 4:8, 2 Chronicles 15:2). Again, we find the complementarity of truth.

I am deeply grieved at the loss of our Christian culture, our Christian consensus. I grieve at the shallowness of American Christianity, the lack of zeal for gospel holiness. I am burdened that so many who profess the gospel live no differently from those who profess no faith at all. I continue to pray and labor for the gospel to penetrate the smug New Englander, the proud Connecticut Yankee, but nothing short of a revival that will use some means to humble and crush our people, to strip away their false bravado, will cause the "wise and intelligent" to come to Jesus for refuge. And you too are seeing the same smugness and lack of hunger for the gospel in your own community. Do you grieve over it? Are you burdened for a once great civilization that continues to wallow in the folly of unbelief? I may not live to see the day, but unless God intervenes powerfully in our nation, I fear that we will be a Muslim nation within a generation or two. You may not see it either, but your children and your grandchildren will, and then what will that mean for them? Has the white man's gospel time "come and gone?" What is to come of this once great nation, founded so surely on Biblical principles, which has prospered due to them, which in her smugness, has long since rejected them? Do you have any of the angst of Jeremiah and Habakkuk who grieved over the lost culture of Judah, who in her pride and arrogance, went her own way into degradation and judgment? Do you weep over our lost condition? Is it intolerable to you?

The Spirit, Grace, and Chastisement

Moses struck the rock twice and water poured forth.

NUMBERS 20:7

O BEDIENCE AND FAITH BRING power while disobedience and lack of faith yield impotence. When Israel continued to grumble and complain against God while in the wilderness, demanding water, accusing Moses of bringing them into the wilderness only to kill them, both Moses and Aaron fell on their faces before God. The glory of the Lord came upon them, and God told Moses to pick up Aaron's rod and speak to the rock and water would flow. Moses struck the rock twice and indeed the water did flow forth from the rock, bestowing life-giving refreshment to the people and their flocks. But God then told Moses that due to his unbelief he would not enter the Promised Land, that God would only allow him to look into it from Mt. Pisgah. So God took Moses to the top of Mt. Pisgah for a look into Canaan, and Moses died shortly thereafter.

Why would God seemingly deal so harshly with Moses? In Exodus 7, in the midst of the ten plagues where Yahweh was manifesting His power over against that of Pharaoh, God told Moses to take his rod—the one that had turned into a snake, the one he would later use to part the waters so that Israel could pass through and Pharaoh and his army drowned—and strike the waters of the Nile. They turned to blood. Moses' rod was one of authority, power, and judgment. Later, after the exodus, when Israel first began their grumbling God told Moses to take his rod of power, judgment, and authority and strike the rock. Water flowed to give life and refreshment to the people. We are told in 1 Corinthians 10 that the rock Moses struck was Christ. We know from Ezekiel 36 and 47, and John 7 that water symbolizes the Holy Spirit's presence and power. Isaiah tells us that Christ was pierced for our transgressions, crushed for our iniquities, that the chastening for our well being fell upon Him, that by His scourging we are healed. Moses striking the rock in Exodus 17 portrays Christ smitten for our sin, taking judgment upon Himself in His death. The death of Christ brings life and refreshment to all who partake in faith of our Rock and Redeemer, the Holy One of Israel, our Savior, (Isaiah 43, Psalm 19).

But the Rock was only to be smitten one time. Moses was instructed in Numbers 20 to take Aaron's rod, the one which budded, a priestly rod and merely speak to the rock. Speaking was all that was necessary. The water would flow because Christ has been struck by the rod of judgment. The priestly work of Christ would suffice. Christ died for sins, once for all, the just for the unjust, in order that He might bring us to God, being put to death in the flesh, but made alive in the Spirit, 1 Peter 3:18. Since Christ has been raised from the dead, death shall no longer be master over Him, Romans 6:8ff.

God chastised Moses because of his disobedience and lack of faith. He refused to allow him to enter Canaan. Yet in his unbelief God was still gracious. Israel, in spite of their grumbling in unbelief, still received the water they needed. Moses still saw the Promised Land from Mt. Pisgah.

So, what does this mean for you? Obedience and faith yield power while disobedience and unbelief bring impotence. Okay, you are a Christian. Your sins are forgiven. You know that the Father is directing your life, providing for your every need, preparing a place for you in heaven; and of course, this is all glorious. The water flows from the rock. You have been to Mt. Pisgah. Perhaps, however, you have not entered into Canaan. Why? Unbelief and disobedience, (see Hebrews 4). Jesus tells the lukewarm Laodicean church that because they are lukewarm He will spit them out of His mouth. The Lord disciplines those whom He loves, and He chastens every son whom He receives. We are told the remedy for lukewarmness is repentance. God is gracious to His people, but He also disciplines them for disobedience and unbelief.

I wonder if the lack of Holy Spirit power in our ministries is due to our having struck the rock of Christ when we only needed to speak to Him in His priestly office. I fear that many of us are missing so much of what God has for us. Do you believe Jesus is more powerful than the homosexual and abortion agenda? Do you believe Jesus is more powerful than Islam and western secularism and post-modernism? Do you believe Jesus can transform whole communities, like He did the Roman world shortly after His ascension? I am sure you answer, "Of course He can." But why are we seeing so few conversions, so little progress in righteousness and holiness? Is it not unbelief and disobedience! You have grace. You have forgiveness and eternal life, but you lack power and efficacy in your church. You have grace but you also have chastisement.

The Father told Jesus in that great Messianic Psalm 2, "Ask of Me, and I will surely give the nations as Thine inheritance, the very ends of the earth as Thy possession." The four living creatures and twenty-four elders, when seeing the glorified Christ take the book and break its seals say, "Worthy art Thou to take the book and to break its seals, for Thou wast slain, and didst purchase for God with Thy blood, men from every tongue, tribe, people, and nation," Revelation 5:9–10. It is God's will that the nations be saved, that all the nations flow to Jerusalem. God will accomplish His purpose, but here's the question for you—will you be part of His program or will you merely sit back and watch others engage in Spirit anointed ministry, seeing the nations flow into Zion?

What must you do? First you must see your need. You must come to realize that you are not rich, that you are wretched, miserable, poor, and blind, and naked. You must be arrested from your worldly stupor, being humiliated at your sinful unbelief and worldliness. You must then repent. You must think differently about yourself, the world, and the ministry of the Father, Son, and Holy Spirit. You must then act differently, seeking God in earnest prayer, turning from acts and attitudes of sin, grieving over your impotence and coldness of heart. And then you must believe that God will do what He says He will do. Ask Him for the salvation of souls, for the healing of marriages, for the reconciling of people within churches. A son, who is instructed by his father to cut the grass and is out of gasoline, need not be reluctant to ask his father for it. He knows it is his father's will for him to cut the grass and he will supply him all he needs to do the work. How much more true is this with the salvation of the nations! Ask, seek, knock and believe the door will be opened to you. Consciously obey God in His commands, and when you fail, quickly repent. Expect Him to do great and mighty things.

Three Affirmations, Three Denials

Son of man, can these bones live?

EZEKIEL 37:3

THE REVIVAL ON THE Isle of Lewis, off the coast of Scotland, from 1949 until 1952 was a remarkable outpouring of the Holy Spirit, bringing conversion to many in all the various towns of that secluded island. God wonderfully used the preaching of Duncan Campbell to break the hearts of these moral, church-going people. Though they almost all attended church and though the men, saved and unsaved alike, led their families in morning and evening devotional times, many were not yet in Christ. God worked powerfully to change them.[76] At the same time Billy Graham was preaching in Los Angeles and the new evangelicalism came from it, replacing the old fundamentalism which was perceived as negative, separatist, and anti-intellectual. Carl F.H. Henry, Harold J. Ockenga, Martyn Lloyd-Jones, Bill Bright, and Francis Schaeffer were also major players in the movement. Though these men disagreed on secondary issues liked Calvinism and Arminianism, church polity, mode of baptism, and eschatology they all agreed on two major doctrines—the inerrancy of Scripture and the vicarious, penal atonement of Christ.

Times have changed drastically since then. David Wells, in his book, *The Courage to be Protestant*, has noted that evangelicalism is fragmented, divided into three camps.[77] The first is the traditional evangelical who still believes in inerrancy and penal atonement. He is driven by theological considerations above everything else. However two new strands of evangelicals have arisen in recent years. The first is the church growth, seeker friendly movement. Bill Hybels is the major architect of the movement,

76. C. and M. Peckham, *Sounds from Heaven: The Revival on the Isle of Lewis, 1949–1952*, 37ff.

77. Wells, *The Courage to be Protestant: Truth-lovers, Marketers, and Emergents in the Postmodern World*, 2.

and it is pragmatically driven. As long as something works, gets results, then use it. There is little concern for tradition or theological considerations in the seeker friendly movement. The second, however, is much more cutting edge, and I suggest much more dangerous. It is the emerging church movement that is very sensitive to the post-modern mind. Since post-modernism denies any final, absolute truth, the emerging church folks are prone to get their theology from their community instead of Scripture. For example, some have said, "Who are we to be so bold as to think we know the mind of God on such issues as women's ordination, abortion, or gay rights."

Our tendency in the evangelical movement, since the late 1940s, (see George Marsden's book *Reforming Fundamentalism*) is to want to sit at the table with the scholars of our world.[78] Far too many have compromised evangelical theology in order to sit at that table. The same is happening today in a sincere effort to relate to and reach the baby boomer and Gen-Xer. We see this even in churches that historically have embraced the Reformed and Calvinistic doctrines of God's sovereignty, man's total inability, and Christ's lordship over His church.

If you have any doubt about the inability of man and the sovereignty of God then study carefully the vision of the valley of dry bones in Ezekiel 37. In his vision Ezekiel sees bones, dry as dust, bleached in the desert sun, spring to life with muscle, sinew, and breath. Clearly the vision is an encouragement to Judah to believe in better days, that God will save a multitude of people, moving them from death to life, from darkness to light, from slavery to sin to freedom in Christ.

Many pastors and church leaders I know are terribly discouraged in ministry. They have tried the latest silver bullet and it has not worked. They are disillusioned, dismayed, and disappointed. It seems that many are simply going through the motions, waiting for the day they can retire or go to another church. May I suggest three affirmations and three denials, which if embraced and applied, can go a long way toward encouraging the discouraged pastor or Elder? *First, affirm God's sovereignty and deny man's autonomy*, (see Isaiah 25:1, Psalm 115:3, Romans 3:10ff). God is absolutely, without equivocation, all powerful and sovereign. He foreordains all that comes to pass. Man is not in control of anything, certainly not his eternal destiny. We say we believe these things but we tend to do another, living

---

78. Marsden, *Reforming Fundamentalism: Fuller Seminary and the New Evangelicalism*, 170.

as *de facto* deists. Deism taught that God created all things, but then leaves man to work everything out the best he can. Benjamin Franklin was a Deist and his adage, "God helps those who help themselves" fits this nicely. Most today, who believe in some vague notion of God will say, "I must do all I can to gain God's favor, and trust Him to do the rest."[79] He must make everything happen from that point forward. So, as *de facto* deists we tend to think we can fix any problem, whether marriage, addiction to drugs, or pornography by some *how-to* program or pill. *Second, affirm man's total inability and deny semi-Pelagianism,* (see Ezekiel 37:1ff, Romans 5:6–8). By man's total inability we mean unregenerate man cannot believe on Christ through his own efforts. He is dead in his sins. He does not seek for God. He is nothing but dry bones in a valley. By semi-Pelagianism we mean modern day Arminianism that denies the doctrine of original sin, believing man has the ability within himself to respond to the gospel. We are in trouble today because we say one thing and do another, living as de facto social engineers. When Bill Hybels admitted last year that his model of ministry had not worked, that his people were ignorant of the Bible, he was man enough to acknowledge his error.[80] However his remedy was built on the same false premise. In order to see what to do next his staff would conduct another survey to see what people want. Should he not instead simply look at Scripture and receive his marching orders from it? A social engineer has an agenda. He will make people in his own image. We fall into this in ministry when we believe man holds the trump card, that he decides for or against Christ. The moment we do this (and evangelicalism since the early nineteenth century has been built on this premise) we are open to programs, music, and all manner of persuasive tactics to get results. While many of these churches are growing numerically they seem largely to be failing in discipling and promoting biblical holiness in their people. Clearly semi-Pelagianism is not working. The church of Christ in America today seems weaker than it has been in years.

And third, affirm the Lordship of Christ and deny missional manipulation, (see 1 Corinthians 3:6, 1 Corinthians 2:1–5). We don't need to worry about numbers or how many are attending church, though lack of conver-

---

79. I am indebted to Steve Bateman for this idea, found in his book *Which Real Jesus? Jonathan Edwards, Benjamin Franklin, and the Early American Roots of the Current Debate,* 34ff.

80. www.blog.christianitytoday.com as reported by the Jude 3 Project, October 18, 2007.

sions ought to break our hearts. We don't need to lament the rise of Islam. Christ's church will not go out of business. She will continue to grow and embrace the nations because God is the One who calls His elect for whom Christ died into union with Him. So we don't need to manipulate or coerce people to attend church by dumbing down our preaching, omitting hard sayings of sin and judgment and the call to holy living. We need to preach and teach in the power of the Holy Spirit, trusting Christ to build His church in His time, in His way. I'm not saying we have a license for laziness or shoddy work. I'm not denying our need for structure, planning, and strategy. I am saying, however, that our confidence is in the Lord, not in man or our devices to reach him.

1735

Do not grieve the Holy Spirit of God with whom you were sealed until the day of redemption.

Ephesians 4:30

1735 was a most remarkable year in the expansion of Christ's kingdom. In order to appreciate what God did that year, we need to go back to 1662 when King Charles II, in an effort to rid England, Scotland, and Wales of Protestantism, required all ministers to submit to Anglicanism, meaning among other things the necessity of affirming the King of England as the head of the church. Charles' desire was to move England to Roman Catholicism.[81] When the Puritan ministers—Anglican, Congregational, and Presbyterian alike, refused, then two thousand were expelled from their pulpits, many of them living in poverty, some dying in prison. Very quickly the Puritan revolution was over and England, Scotland, Wales, and America fervently embraced Deism, a denial of the supernatural and imminent work of God in the lives of people. All manner of debauchery ruled the day in the early eighteenth century, the time which gave us the Scottish and French Enlightenment championed by such skeptics as David Hume, Voltaire, and Rousseau. But people were praying for a fresh outpouring of the Holy Spirit, like what had happened in the mid 1600s in Scotland and New England. The Scottish Covenanters, who were suffering severe persecution and death in the 1680s, led the way in prayer. Nothing seemed to be happening for over fifty years until 1735. In Northampton, Massachusetts young Jonathan Edwards had followed his grandfather Solomon Stoddard as the pastor of the Congregational Church there, and he began to see a remarkable interest in the gospel, resulting in hundreds

81. He had secretly converted to Roman Catholicism, and on his deathbed received the Roman Catholic Eucharist. Fraser, *Royal Charles: Charles II and the Restoration*, 451ff.

of people being converted in the first six months of 1735. In January of that year, Sarah, Edwards' wife who had been a Christian since childhood, experienced a fresh moving of the Spirit in her life, enabling her to overcome a spiritual depression that had plagued her for years. Meanwhile in Wales twenty-one year old Howell Harris came under conviction of his sin, and was converted a few weeks after Easter. In June he experienced an outpouring of the Spirit in his life which gave him the boldness, zeal, and efficacy to become a marvelous evangelistic preacher. At the same time, Daniel Rowland, an Anglican minister in Wales, came under conviction of his sin through the preaching Welsh evangelist Griffith Jones. His conversion led him to continue his pastoral ministry for another forty years, but with a new, evangelistic zeal. And around Easter of 1735 young George Whitefield, a member of the Holy Club at Oxford with John and Charles Wesley, all of whom were serious and zealous in their religion, came to see that his zeal was without life. After some serious soul searching, he too came to peace with God through Jesus Christ. He soon became the greatest itinerant evangelist since the Apostle Paul, preaching throughout England, Scotland, and Wales, up and down the Atlantic seaboard in Colonial America, to as many as fifty thousand people at one time in the open air, without the aid of voice amplification. God brought the Great Awakening, which many have said saved Great Britain and America from the ravages of the French Revolution, through Whitefield, Harris, Edwards, and Rowland.

Those, like me, in the Reformed tradition of evangelicalism have a great heritage, yet it is one, I fear, we have forsaken. The great Puritan John Owen, in volume three of his sixteen volumes on theology, wrote nearly seven hundred pages on the Holy Spirit.[82] Our Reformed church history is replete with evidence of the outpouring of the Holy Spirit, resulting in great joy, power, holiness, transformation of cultures, and building up of the body of Christ. We tend to live like *de facto* deists, believing in God, but denying His day to day activity in our lives. My brethren, these things ought not to be. Paul is commanding us not to grieve, not to send away, not to bring sorrow to the Holy Spirit. This anthropopathism (there are others, see Exodus 34:6, James 4:5) tells us that we can lose the presence and power of the Holy Spirit in our lives. The same idea is intimated in Song of Songs 5:1ff where the groom (a picture of Christ) covers himself with myrrh (a sweet fragrance), eats honey (the sweetness of the word),

---

82. Owen, *The Works of John Owen, volume 3, The Holy Spirit.*

and drinks wine (the joy of Christ) and comes to his bride (the church). She is waiting for him but when he comes she says, "I am already in bed, and my feet are washed. I cannot come to the door." When she calls out for him he is gone. When she searches for him she cannot find him. We can lose the presence and power of the Holy Spirit.

How does this happen? Four things come immediately to mind. One, when we do anything unholy, anything contrary to the clear commands of God, then He may choose to leave us, (see Isaiah 59:1–2). Two, when we forget His presence, when we live as though He does not see what we do, then He may leave us, (see Psalm 51:10–12). Three, when we ignore His promptings, when He prompts us to pray, to call someone, to witness the gospel to someone, and we do not do it, then He may leave us, (see 1 Thessalonians 5:19). And four, the Holy Spirit may leave us when we fail to live with our final redemption in view. The Preacher in Ecclesiastes vividly describes the vanity of those who live "under the sun," failing to acknowledge that our great God will bring a final restoration of all things on that great day.

What results from grieving, bringing sorrow to the Holy Spirit? First, you will not lose your salvation. You will not lose the indwelling Holy Spirit, and you will not be abandoned by God. However you will lose the sense of His presence. It will feel as though God has deserted you. You will lose a deep, abiding sense of His love for you. And when this happens you will forfeit joy, peace, power, joy, and assurance of God's blessing and direction in your life. Furthermore, you will open yourself up to the machinations of the world, flesh, and devil. Your weaknesses will be exposed to these great enemies of your soul, and they will exploit them, not unlike what the Nazi's did in December 1944 at the Battle of the Bulge when they attacked a weak spot in the Allied line in Belgium. What then are you to do? Two things come to mind. First, you must believe in the Holy Spirit. I know you say you believe in Him, but I fear most of us pay Him lip service only. He is the third person of the Godhead and you can grieve, quench, or resist Him. He alone is the one who creates (Genesis 1), re-creates (Titus 3:5), comforts (John 14:26), exalts Christ (John 16:24), sanctifies (Galatians 5:22ff), and empowers (Ephesians 5:18ff). Second, you must repent daily, many times per day. You ought to repent even when you cannot think of specific sins you have committed. The Spirit is rich in mercy, and will come to you quickly when you humble yourself before Him. Will you believe in the Holy Spirit? Ask God to make you sensitive to your sin, so sensitive that you immediately come to Jesus in repentance when you feel the slightest estrangement from Him. Without this, you will make no progress in revival living.

The Pledge of the Holy Spirit

... who is given as a pledge of our inheritance, with a view to the redemp-
tion of God's own possession, to the praise of His glory.

EPHESIANS 1:14

JOHN MILTON, PERHAPS THE second most important poet (William Shakespeare, of course, being the first) in England's history, was born in 1608 at the height of the Puritan revolution, a mighty movement of God in Scotland, England, and Wales. Milton's father had come to Christ in the late 1500's, and sought to rear his children in the nurture and admonition of the Lord. By the time John Milton was nine years old he was fluent in Greek and Latin, and at the age of seventeen entered Christ's College, Cambridge, where upon graduation he stayed on a few more years to tutor younger students, one of whom was Roger Williams, the Baptist who came to America and founded Providence, Rhode Island. Milton also became fluent in Hebrew, French, and Italian, traveling to Europe where he conversed with an aging Galileo. Milton married at the age of thirty-three but his young wife, sixteen year old Mary Powell, left him after the first month of their marriage. Apparently she preferred the comforts of momma and daddy to the quiet, perhaps even boring life of an austere, Puritan scholar. They were estranged for three years but finally reconciled, Mary bearing Milton four children. Mary died after the birth of the fourth, and a few days later their fifteen month old son died too. Milton remarried three years later. His second wife, Katharine, and their child both died from complications of the labor and delivery. Milton married a third time. Elizabeth cared for him until his death in 1674. Milton rarely had any money. His financial pressures were enormous. Then there was the issue of siding with the Puritans during the Cromwellian Protectorate, meaning that after Cromwell died in 1658, Charles II, who was restored to the throne of England, punished the Puritan leaders, including John Milton. On top of all this, Milton became blind by his mid forties. He constantly battled bitterness and depression, but by the end of his life he was filled with the wonder of Christ's love for him and hope of heaven.

John Milton came to understand and apply the marvelous truth in Ephesians 1:14, the pledge, down payment, or earnest of the Holy Spirit. We find this concept of the Holy Spirit given as a pledge in 2 Corinthians 1:22, 5:5. The inheritance to which Paul is referring is mentioned numerous other places (Romans 8:17, Acts 20:32), and is the believer's full and final redemption. In Ephesians 1:7 and Colossians 1:14 Paul speaks of redemption, and has in mind what happens at the moment the death of Christ is applied to one by the Holy Spirit, meaning that the blood of Christ purchases our ransom from sin and death. But redemption also has a fuller, more eschatological meaning, looking to the day when all true believers will receive their reward—heaven and the new earth, (see Ephesians 4:30, Luke 21:28, Romans 8:23). Paul concludes all three sections of his doxology in Ephesians 1:6, 12, 14 by declaring that the work of salvation by the Father, Son, and Holy Spirit is all to the praise and glory of His grace.

Here's what Paul means—the present work of the Holy Spirit in the believer, His calling, convicting, regenerating, converting, justifying, sanctifying, adopting, comforting, and teaching all serve as a down payment or pledge (like putting down earnest money when making a real estate transaction) to encourage us to look to the future when we will receive the full and complete inheritance—eternal life in the presence of Jesus, the perfecting of a glorified body, the new heaven and the new earth.

We need desperately this down payment of future glory, not because God is deficient, but because the circumstances of life erode our faith. Was this not the case with John Milton? No doubt this is the case with you too. The relentless storms of life can work steadily to erode the foundation of faith. Is this happening to you? Perhaps it is if you see no hope out of your circumstances, if you are merely "clocking in" at work, in your marriage, with your children.

What's the remedy? You need to assess your situation. Do you see evidence of effectual calling, regeneration, conversion, justification, sanctification? Are you aware of God's chastisement, His discipline, at times in your life? He disciplines every son whom He loves. Use this first fruit, this earnest of your inheritance, to remind you that your full and final redemption is drawing near. Realize that it won't be long before you see

Jesus face to face, and the glory that awaits you is completely beyond your comprehension.

Milton, by the time he was in his forties, was blind, but it was then that he began his magnum opus, *Paradise Lost*. He would begin each day at five a.m., having the Hebrew Bible read to him for an hour. He would then dictate his poem. He would break for an hour walk, relax by playing the viola or organ for an hour, and then begin work again until evening. The result was a masterpiece and the work transformed him.

Dear believer, consider your great inheritance, of which the present work of the Holy Spirit is a mere foretaste. In Acts 7 Stephen is making his defense before the Sanhedrin, and in rage they stone him to death. As he is dying, Luke tells us that he was filled with the Holy Spirit, that he gazed into heaven and saw the glory of God, with Jesus standing at the right hand of God. In most cases in the New Testament we read of Jesus sitting at the right hand of God, a picture of His exaltation and eternal session. But now He is standing as He receives Stephen. When a judge enters his courtroom, those present stand. When the President of the United States enters Congress or a press conference all present stand as a show of respect for his office. When a guest comes to your home you rise and welcome him, a sign of graciousness. The Lord Jesus, who died for you, who has given you the down payment of the Holy Spirit, is promising you a full and final redemption. He will stand to receive you into heaven on that day when you close your eyes in death. Sometimes this does not excite us because we love the world so much. But sooner or later you will be broken by the world; and when you are then heaven will be all the more glorious to you. Until that time, hold on, don't grow weary, lift up your head, straighten up for your redemption is drawing near. Jesus will stand to welcome you into His glorious presence. Do not grow weary. Apply the Spirit's presence as your pledge of future glory.

Honor the Holy Ghost

... the mystery of Christ ... as it has now been revealed ... in the Spirit.

EPHESIANS 3:5

D.L. MOODY, THE great nineteenth century evangelist, was born in Northfield, Massachusetts and, due to his family's poverty, received only a third grade education. As a teen Moody moved to Boston and became a shoe salesman, hearing the gospel from another worker, and being wonderfully converted. Immediately Moody began to work with the local YMCA in preaching the gospel to children. He later moved to Chicago, and did the same thing with increasing notoriety. There were two Methodist women who often attended Moody's meetings, who afterward would say, "We are praying for you Mr. Moody." After hearing this several times, Moody, a bit miffed, asked them, "Why are you praying for me? Why don't you pray for the conversion of the lost?" They said that they were praying for Moody to receive the power. Moody began to pray with these women and a few months later, while walking down Wall Street in Manhattan, a few days before his departure for London and evangelistic preaching, the power came upon him. He says that he was so overcome with the glory and power of the Holy Spirit that he thought he may die on the spot. He immediately went to the house of a nearby friend and spent several hours in a bedroom, communing with God. D.L. Moody's ministry was never the same after this baptism with the Holy Spirit. He became a powerful and useful preacher of the gospel in England, Scotland, and America, being responsible, in a human sense, for the conversion of thousands of people and for the establishment of three schools. From that point onward Moody always said that we must honor the Holy Ghost.[83]

In light of the fact that only one percent of Connecticut where I live is evangelical and sixteen percent claim to be atheist or agnostic, since

83. Torrey, *Why God Used D. L. Moody*, 45.

only eight percent of Americans are evangelical,[84] in light of the erosion of a Biblical consensus through modernism and post modernism, and since the denomination of which I am a part, the Presbyterian Church in America, has grown by only one percent in recent years, surely we ought to be asking ourselves the question—do we have the power? Should we not be praying earnestly for Holy Ghost power in our pulpit ministries and churches?

Paul in Ephesians 3:5 says that the mystery of Christ—His promised incarnation, humiliation, and exaltation for the sins of His people, has now been revealed to His holy apostles and prophets in the Spirit. In other words, the Holy Spirit is the One who called, equipped, and empowered the New Testament apostles and prophets to preach Christ crucified, opening the eyes of the blind to see the light of Christ. God has since called men to preach Christ crucified to the nations, drawing millions to Himself through the convicting and regenerating work of the Holy Spirit. It ought to be clear to us that the presence and power of the Holy Spirit is essential to Biblical ministry in the church and world. I fear, however, that most of us merely pay lip service to His ministry, foolishly thinking, in our pride and professionalism, that our plans, programs, and personalities will promote prosperity in ministry.

Who is the Holy Spirit? Since He clearly has divine perfections, should we not, therefore, confess Him to be God? He is omnipotent (1 Corinthians 12:11), omniscient (Isaiah 40:13–14), omnipresent (Psalms 139:7–10), and He is eternal (Hebrews 9:14). Should we not, therefore, honor Him? What does He do? Consider His work of creation (Psalm 33:6), preparation (Luke 1:35), inspiration (2 Peter 1:21), regeneration (Titus 3:5), resurrection (Romans 8:11), application (1 Corinthians 12:13), sanctification (Romans 1:4), and formation (Ephesians 1:22–23). And what do we mean by the Spirit's presence and power? I mean two things. First is His ordinary presence. The Holy Spirit indwells all believers, powerfully working regeneration and sanctification in them, bringing conviction of sin and comfort in times of sorrow. But second is His extraordinary presence where He does something far more dynamic that the ordinary. This ought to be the norm in our churches but sadly it is not. Thus I reluctantly call this the extraordinary work of the Spirit. Acts 4:31 is a case in point where the place they were gathered was shaken and they were filled with the Holy

---

84. Barna Group, www.barna.org, August 23, 2005.

Spirit, speaking the word of God with great boldness. The awe filled presence at Enfield, Connecticut in July 1741 when Jonathan Edwards preached his famous sermon, *Sinners In The Hands Of An Angry God*;[85] and the felt presence of God in 1949[86] on the Isle of Lewis in the Outer Hebrides off the coast of Scotland are both examples of the extraordinary presence of the Holy Spirit.

And why is the presence of the Holy Spirit so needed in our day? Why is He so essential for our ministries? I give four reasons. *First is the depravity of the sinner* (Romans 3:10ff). Man cannot and will not come to Christ through any coercion or manipulation that Pelagian or Arminian preachers bring. I, for one, am not at all impressed by the rock and roll, mega churches of our day that claim to be mighty movements of God. They are fundamentally flawed at the beginning, working on the dreadful assumption that man holds the cards, that man has the ability to decide for Christ, and that the evangelist's job is to find the key to his heart. Pastor, church leader, do you really believe in the total inability of people to believe the gospel? Are you praying with total dependence upon God, clearing the sinful debris from your life and church so that the Holy Spirit may come with awe filled power upon your ministry? *Second is the frailty of the saint.* The very thing we wish to do we do not do, and the thing we do not want to do, we do (Romans 7:15ff). You cannot grow in holiness without the Holy Spirit's sanctifying work. *And third is the fact that the church is prone to folly.* Paul rebuked the Corinthians in his severe letter (2 Corinthians 7), probably because they did not come to his defense when falsely accused. We continue to go after the folly of fads and formulas, forgetting what we already know— that only the Holy Spirit can convert and sanctify. *And fourth, those in the world are prone to pride, unbelief, and rebellion.* Do we not see this today in New England? People generally reject Christianity because they do not see it as relevant or because it is found wanting in intellectual rigor. Pride in our plans and programs takes us away from God and our lust fastens us to the world and its methods.

What, then, are you to do? You are to honor the Holy Ghost. How? Believe in Him. Jesus told His disciples to wait in Jerusalem until they were clothed with power from on high (Luke 24:46ff, Acts 1:8). Do you believe in the Holy Ghost? Do you really believe in Him? Are you truly

85. Marsden, *Jonathan Edwards: A Life*, 220.

86. See *Sounds from Heaven: The Revival on the Isle of Lewis, 1949–1952* by Colin and Mary Peckham, 92.

desperate for Him? Have you come to see your need of Him in your ministry and family? Do you really expect the Holy Spirit to convict people of sin and to regenerate them? Second you must seek Him. Be filled with the Spirit (Ephesians 5:18), do not grieve the Spirit (Ephesians 4:30), do not quench the Spirit (1 Thessalonians 5:19), and do not resist the Spirit (Acts 7:51). Will you honor the Holy Ghost?

It's Time for Revival Prayer

*So I contended with them and cursed them and struck some of them
and pulled out their hair.*

NEHEMIAH 13:25

AFTER HEARING OF THE devastation in Jerusalem and consequently
praying and fasting, Nehemiah moves to Jerusalem to repair the wall
around the city. Later he hears that the men of the covenant are giving
their sons to foreign women and their daughters to foreign men. He con-
tends with them, pronounces curses upon them, hits some of them, and
pulls out their hair. For whom do you feel compassion in this story? If
you answer, "Those being abused by Nehemiah," then you are part of the
problem of the church in our nation. Nehemiah, Ezra, and Daniel were all
devastated by the sin of the covenant people. After all, Yahweh had a long
history of blessing His people, going back to the days of Abraham, and later in their deliverance from Egyptian bondage at the hands of Moses. He
continually warned them of the consequences of playing the harlot with
foreign gods, eventually bringing destruction upon both the northern and
southern kingdoms. However, in a remarkable work of grace He returned
them to their land at the hands of Cyrus of the Medo-Persian Empire.
Indeed, Yahweh was good to His people. And how did His people reward
His beneficence? They continued to play the harlot, giving their children
to godless pagans. No wonder Nehemiah and Ezra tore their own hair
from their heads and beards, not to mention that of the perpetrators!

"An astonishing and horrible thing has happened in the land. The
prophets prophesy falsely, the priests rule according to their desires, and
My people love it so. But what will happen at the end of it?" (Jeremiah
5:20–21). Though wonderfully blessed by the true and living God, we
have continually turned away from Him, thus provoking Him to wrath.
I suggest at least three national sins that threaten to destroy us. The first
is pride, "I know what is best, and I do what I want." Pride reveals itself,

among many other things, in our sexual sins. We are a culture given over to fornication, adultery, pornography, pedophilia, and homosexuality. The second is greed, "I want what others have. I deserve it, even though I choose not to work for it." Greed is rampant on Wall Street with CEO's sacrificing long term, respectable financial growth for a short term profit that inflates their stock options and leaves the employees with little to nothing. Greed is rampant on Main Street with a growing welfare, redistribution of wealth ethos. I am not simply speaking of the Democrats. Many leading Republicans also pushed through the 2008 bail-out packages. And third is unbelief, "I don't believe what God's word says." This has left us with religious pluralism and the Islamanization of the west. British schools have removed references to the holocaust from their text books. What is the reason? Muslims are offended by the holocaust, saying it never happened.[87] Wherever Christianity has flourished (the Middle East, North Africa, and Europe) Islam has eventually overcome it or is in the process of doing so. Why? We have given ourselves over to folly. We have turned away from devotion to the true and living God, of humbling ourselves under His mighty hand; and instead we have spread our legs to every suitor (Ezekiel 16:25) who passes by. God is not mocked. Whatever a man sows, this he will also reap. God will by no means leave the guilty unpunished. He is a jealous and avenging God.

Our greatest evil, however, the very fountainhead of all our sin is abortion. It is the root of our pride, greed, and unbelief. If I were a black man, I would be doubly incensed by the godless in our land who foist it upon us. That's because, in keeping with Margaret Sanger's (originator of Planned Parenthood)[88] racist and bigoted statements about black people (they read like something out of the KKK), the black race is currently being decimated by abortion (one thousand per day, fifteen million of the forty-four million abortions in America).[89]

Abortion is fueled by pride because people use it as birth control. "I can live as I want, and if I become pregnant, then I will simply have an abortion." It is fueled by greed. Some say, "I don't want a baby right now. This will interfere with my career, the travel I wish to do." And it is fueled by unbelief. Only ten percent of Downs Syndrome babies are born today.

87. www.islamonline.net, April 5, 2007.

88. George Grant, in his book, *Grand Illusions: The Legacy of Planned Parenthood* explores this notion in great detail, 57.

89. Gardner, "More and More Black Babies Murdered Via Abortion," *The Hick Town Press.*

That's because people deny the authority of God who says that all life is precious, that He is sovereign in all the affairs of life, that He makes no mistakes, even in giving certain women children with birth defects.

What are we to do? We are not to circle the wagons, to act as though the world is so evil that we must retreat from it, protecting ourselves from its evil influences. Instead we must take the word of God and the light of Christ to those who live in such darkness. Preachers must preach, getting the word of truth into as many people as they possibility can. I urge preachers to take every opportunity they can to teach and preach the word of God. I urge lay people to learn the Bible and start Bible studies in their neighborhoods and places of work. And then we must call people to faith in Christ. We need a holy boldness to take the gospel to a culture drunk on the blood of the innocents, a people satiated with lasciviousness, to a greedy nation that worships Mammon, exchanging the truth of God for a lie. I am not naïve, however. Many of you will not pray, and fewer of you will take the gospel boldly to your communities. I know your unbelieving communities hate God and want nothing of biblical Christianity. I have been in the ministry long enough to know that the last thing most of us want to do is to pray and evangelize.

What are we to do then? We need to ask God to give us a burden for revival prayer. We need to be brought low, to be devastated, grief stricken, to gain a deep sense of corporate guilt and condemnation for the sins of our nation. We need to feel the wrath of God against us for our rebellion against His mercies. We need, as it were, to pull out our hair, even that of believers who so easily continue in grievous sin. When we are deeply moved, devastated, then and only then will we pray revival prayers. Revival prayers are different from prayers for revival. The latter are nice, short, calm prayers we lift up to God. They salve our consciences, and give us the license to say, "Well, I prayed for revival, and God did not do anything. I guess His will is no revival." Revival prayer is what the Chinese, Korean, and Sudanese Christians do, who live with the threat of destruction and persecution. Their circumstances have become intolerable to them, and they cannot help but cry out to God for mercy and power. There is earnestness, steadfastness, desperateness in their prayers. They pray for long periods of time (often all night, all day, for many days) confessing their sins, praying with a clear sense that unless the Lord builds the house, they labor in vain who build it. Without this kind of prayer and God's consequent outpouring of mass conversions, the west will be Muslim in fifty years. I hope I am wrong but history says otherwise.

What If?

Be filled with the Holy Spirit.

<small>EPHESIANS 5:18</small>

IN JULY 1997 MY wife and I had the privilege of taking tea with Lord and Lady Catherwood in Cambridge, England. Lady Catherwood is the daughter of my favorite preacher, Martyn Lloyd-Jones, who so ably preached the doctrines of grace, beginning in Aberavon, Wales in 1927 and concluding shortly before his death on March 1, 1981. I was able to ask Lady Catherwood a series of questions about her father and his ministry. One of my questions had to do with the revival they experienced at the little Presbyterian Church in Aberavon. She said that she was only a young child when it began but she distinctly remembered the presence of God. She said it was glorious and she has never forgotten it. During this ministry a well known spirit-medium wandered into the church one Sunday evening, on her way to a séance. She listened to the sermon and continued to return, eventually being soundly converted out of witchcraft to faith in Christ. When Lloyd-Jones asked her about attending for the first time, she said that she sensed a clean spirit was present.[90]

The church of Jesus in the west today reminds me of a state-of-the-art manufacturing plant, having a beautiful building, an experienced and gifted leadership and staff, the latest in information systems, and the best research and development of any competitor. There is only one thing missing—electricity. A plant without electricity is going nowhere. The church has her buildings, theologically trained professional ministers, staff, and a plethora of programs, but we lack power. We lack Holy Ghost power. What would happen if everyone in your church was drunk, as it were, with the Holy Spirit?

---

90. Murray, *D. Martyn Lloyd-Jones: The First Forty Years, 1899–1939,* 221.

Paul is giving the Ephesians two commands in this passage—one is negative (do not get drunk with wine for that is unsavableness, literally the Greek word means this), and the other is positive (be being filled with the Holy Spirit). Paul follows this present tense, imperative with five present tense participles that describe the nature of being filled—speaking to one another in psalms, hymns, spiritual songs; singing and making melody in our hearts to the Lord; giving thanks to the Father through Christ; and being subject to one another in the fear of Christ.

What does it mean to be filled with the Spirit? Consider one who is drunk with wine. He thinks, speaks, acts, feels, walks differently. Why? Because he is under the influence of alcohol. Similarly one filled or dominated by the Holy Spirit thinks, speaks, acts, feels, and walks like God. To be more specific, he does what the Holy Spirit does, (see John 14:16, 16:26, Titus 3:5). The Holy Spirit exalts Christ, bringing regeneration to people, convicting them of sin, comforting them, causing them to grow in grace, to become more like Jesus. So, one filled with the Spirit, when teaching, preaching, evangelizing, counseling, discipling, showing mercy sees his work *take*. It is effectual. These listeners are not merely people who hear and are partially helped in their marriages, who make professions of faith but persist in their sin, who seemingly never overcome their drug or sexual addictions. When the Spirit regenerates then transformation occurs.

Peter was a man given to the sins of pride, presumption, and cowardice prior to Pentecost, but then, in fulfillment of Joel's prophecy, the Spirit came upon those who had been praying for ten days; and Peter began to preach with unction and boldness, seeing five thousand converted on that day. He never looked back. The outpouring of the Spirit in Acts is normative for the church. We ought to see the same sort of thing happen today. Why don't we? Because we are not filled with the Spirit.

What results from the filling of the Spirit? The first thing is gospel holiness in the form of the fruit of the Spirit (Galatians 5:22–23). Simply put—does your life consistently and progressively show itself in love, joy, peace, patience, kindness, goodness, gentleness, faithfulness, and self-control? Second, observing what we see in Acts, since it is normative, a group of people in one church being filled with the Spirit means that mighty prayer is going on somewhere. It is prayer that grieves over personal sin, where confession and repentance is occurring, where people are energized to pray for long periods of time without interruption, (see Nehemiah 1, Daniel 10, Acts 2). It results in mighty preaching. By that

I mean the preacher proclaims unapologetically the word of God, that people are struck by the solemnity of it, that God has His way with the people, that the people are riveted on the sermon, not thinking about what their team is doing later that day. They know God is speaking directly to them. It results in mighty conversions, not mere professions of faith where we have to run after people to get them into a follow-up program. Instead it yields transformation, a clean break with darkness, a careful walk in the light. It results in mighty assemblies. Yes, even in Presbyterian Churches like the one I serve there is emotion, awe, weeping, confessing, conversions, reconciliation between spouses, reconciliation between children and their parents, friends being reconciled with friends. It results in mighty acts of compassion, where people put away their prejudices against people different than they, and reach out to help them in specific, concrete ways, giving their time and money to serve others. It results in mighty community where believers genuinely love one another, forgive one another, deal kindly with one another, share what they have with one another. It results in mighty generosity where people let go of their money and time, giving it freely, joyously for the sake of the kingdom and the good of people.

Are you seeing this in your church? We at Christ Community Presbyterian Church, West Hartford, Connecticut by the grace of God, are experiencing a taste of it, and it is glorious. It is all of God. I must say, however, that it is only a taste. It is limited. It is not comprehensive. We still have a majority of people who seemingly show up, engage in corporate worship, listen to a sermon, take communion and go home. But there are some with whom God is dealing directly, powerfully, gloriously, effectually.

What if everyone in our church was filled with the Spirit? What if everyone in your church was filled with the Spirit, was dominated and controlled by the One who exalts Jesus, who convicts of sin, righteousness, and judgment, who comforts, who instructs, who empowers for holiness? What does this practically look like in your life, whatever your work and family situation? You pray, walk humbly, and you are quick to confess your sins. You will find an unusual boldness and efficacy in your speech. You will find great joy and expectancy. You simply expect God to save, sanctify, and reconcile people.

Courage

Act like men.

1 CORINTHIANS 16:13

SIMON SCHAMA IN HIS book, *The Embarrassment of Riches*,[91] writes of the golden era of Dutch life, the seventeenth century. The Netherlands at that time, though a very small nation, was a colonial power, the center of the artistic and architectural world, and extremely wealthy. Schama chronicles how the Dutch Calvinistic preachers continually drew parallels between the Netherlands and Israel as chosen nations of God, and their consequent requirement to be faithful to God's covenant with them, showing that their material, artistic, and military success was due to the hand of God, in response to their zeal in obeying His covenant. Schama seems to dismiss this notion of the fear of God and keeping His covenant as the formula for Dutch success. He views it as a quaint superstition. Can we not, however, see something to this need? We read throughout the Old Testament of God blessing His chosen people Israel, of how He entered into covenant with them, and how He promised blessing if they obeyed Him (see Deuteronomy 28:1ff), and curses if they disobeyed Him (see Deuteronomy 28, 29). It also seems clear that wherever Calvinism has taken root material prosperity follows. Certainly we cannot say that Calvinism is the sole reason for material prosperity because the Enlightenment notion of progress that ushered in the Industrial Revolution also was a major player. And we must also quickly admit that material prosperity can so quickly morph into worldliness and consumerism that has brought us to where we are today in the west, namely what some are calling "cultural nihilism." American nihilism is different from European nihilism. The latter is more philosophical in nature. Think Nietzsche for example. Our own brand of nihilism is illustrated in *Seinfeld*,

---

91. Schama, *The Embarrassment of Riches: An Interpretation of Dutch Culture in the Golden Age,* 133.

a television program by its own admission about nothing, suggesting that life in the world is devoid of any real meaning. I never recall an episode of *Seinfeld* that even hinted at anything serious.

The simple, undeniable fact however, is that obedience to God's law brings prosperity of every kind. Obviously a believer living in a totalitarian or Islamic state or one living in a corrupt, African country, no matter how much he personally seeks to honor God, will be severely limited in his ability to prosper materially. This does not negate what I am saying, rather it further proves it. The leaders of these nations have chosen to disobey God's law with the fruit being poverty and oppression for those not privileged to have their high position. But when a nation makes the God of the Bible their God, when they turn humbly to Him and seek to live righteously, justly, and obediently then her people will prosper. We call this the civil use of the Law of God. The Law of God protects and provides for people. Paul the Apostle commands children in Ephesians 6:2 to honor their fathers and mothers so that they may live long on the earth. A person, for example, who obeys the speed limit is more apt to stay away from automobile accidents. Obviously this is not always true, but the general principle is there as a protection and encouragement.

But what if you have been steeped in sin? What if you have been living a lie? What if you are paralyzed by your sinful rebellion? What if you are terribly discouraged, thinking you cannot pull yourself out of the darkness? What if you are given to self-pity?

Paul's admonition in 1 Corinthians 16:13 fits here. He says, "Act like men." The Lutheran commentator R.C.H. Lenski notes that four imperatives are given in this verse, "Be on the alert, stand firm in the faith, act like men, be strong."[92] These are all in the present tense, meaning this is a command we are always to obey. These four commands strengthen Paul's command in verse 14, "let all that you do be done in love." Here's the remedy for your self-pity, self-inflicted paralysis, and discouragement. Act like a man. Be manly. Suck it up. Do the next thing correctly. Put away your sin. Quit blaming others. Own up to your own responsibilities. Don't be a coward. Face the music. Make restitution.

To repent means to change your mind. Always, in true Biblical repentance, this also means a change in your behavior. I am not Biblically repenting if I tell my wife I am sorry for speaking rudely to her, if I do

92. Lenski, *Commentary on the New Testament: The Interpretation of St. Paul's First and Second Epistles to the Corinthians*, 772ff.

it again tomorrow. To repent means you change the way you think. You begin to hate your sin, every sin, and your actions change too. Perhaps your emotions will follow, and you will feel good about what you have done. But perhaps they will not. Feelings are not the issue.

So why should you act like a man and obey God? Because He is sovereign and He demands it. Because He is loving and His love seeks to move you to it. And because the blood of Jesus shed for you ought to humble you to the dust, moving you earnestly to desire to honor the lover of your soul.

What Would Revival Look Like in Your Town?

I will dwell on a high and holy place, and also with the contrite and lowly
of spirit in order to revive the spirit of the lowly
and to revive the heart of the contrite.

ISAIAH 57:15

A FEW YEARS AGO I preached nine sermons on Revival from various Old Testament passages that record revivals. In these sermons I stressed our need for revival, what revival is, what hinders it, that it is a sovereign work of the Holy Spirit, meaning we cannot produce a revival, but we can and should prepare the way for one. To go further, we should expect revival if we meet one vital obligation. We must be willing to pay the price for it. Our part is to pay the price for revival, namely to repent of sin, to obey God, and to pray fervently for an outpouring of the Spirit.

Recently a church member asked, "If revival came to New England, or more specifically West Hartford, what would it look like? Your historical examples are interesting and inspiring, but what would this look like today in our secular culture when so few people are interested in Christ and His gospel?" That's a fair question and using Old Testament examples, the book of Acts, and the history of revivals as a template, I suggest revival in West Hartford, or your town for that matter, would look something like this.

First is the matter of preparation. God would move people, not necessarily a large number, to pray earnestly for revival, what I call revival prayer. People would be burdened to pray. The condition of the church and culture would be intolerable to them. They must see change. They cry out earnestly to God. They would be serious about repenting of their sin, making restitution to those whom they have wronged, being zealous to right the wrongs they have done to others. They would be very grieved with their sin, and would not rest until they had dealt biblically with all known sin. They, with Nehemiah, Ezra, and Daniel would be very aware of their profound guilt. This would not necessarily be in sins of commis-

158

sion, things we have done against God, since many are outwardly obedient and righteous. Instead it would reveal itself in the guilt of omission, not doing all that God commands us to do. In summary, we would be profoundly aware, humbled to the dust over our failure to love our neighbor as ourselves. Then there would be earnest preaching for and about revival. Preachers would boldly and without compromise call their people to repentance, bearing down very specifically about sin, urging them to be grieved over it, exalting Christ as the only remedy, expecting the Spirit to promote Biblical holiness in the congregation.

Second would be God's sovereign visitation upon His people. By this I mean several things. As the Holy Spirit begins to work in the hearts of God's people there would be public confession of sin along with sincere contrition, and a keen sense of how they have grieved the Holy Spirit and the God of love and grace. They would become indignant about their sin, seeing that they have so easily and casually sinned without regret and remorse. The people would begin separating themselves from their sin. Those things they previously did not consider sin, now would deeply burden them, and they would be very quick to rid their lives of them—things like certain music, television programming, books, places they frequent. They would begin to fear God, being aware of the warnings of Hebrews, realizing how fearful it is to fall into the hands of the living God. They would genuinely love the word of God. They would not be able to get enough of sound, biblical preaching. One sermon a week would not do it for them. They would listen to preaching every day. If meetings were held nightly at the church they would attend, not being able to stay away from them. The word of God would come alive to them. They would feed on the word of God and make the preachers task a great joy because they would be so eager to listen and change their behavior accordingly. They would give themselves to true worship, to the adoration of God. Worship would be a great delight to them, not only corporate worship but also family and personal worship. This would not be a burden or chore rather it would be a joy from the heart. Their lives would be dominated by joy, a sense of God's love for them, and a boldness in speaking to others about Christ and their souls. Their evangelizing, teaching, and counseling would be efficacious. People would listen and change.

And third, this sort of thing happening in the lives of God's people would then begin to impact previously hard-hearted, disinterested, prideful, self-righteous, wicked people. They would be awakened to their perilous condition. They would be fearful of their soul's estate. They would begin to pursue God. Instead of coercing or pleading with them to join you at church or to attend a bible study, they would be hungry for these things. They would see them as vital, of paramount importance. Then many of them would be soundly converted. I don't mean a few here and there who make a decision for Christ, and then you wonder what happened to them, that you never see them again. No, in revival many come to Christ and give clear evidence of sound conversion, turning from darkness to light, from loving sin and hating God to hating sin and loving God. Then this would mean a transformation of families, churches, and communities. It would affect all levels of society—the rich and the poor, the professional and day laborer, all the various ethnic groups in your community. Perhaps the revival would be very quiet and non-emotional, like the ones at Midway, Georgia in the nineteenth century;[93] or perhaps they would be highly charged with emotion like the one at Cambuslang, Scotland in 1742.[94] To put it another way, the normal Christian life to which we are accustomed would, in revival, be supercharged. Instead of one or two conversions, here and there, many would be soundly converted at the same time. It would be the normal Christian life on steroids.

Here's my question to you—do you believe God can do this sort of thing again today? I hope you do. But here's an even more audacious question—do you believe He will? Are you willing to pay the price for revival? I fear that most are not. What is that price? It is revival prayer that begins with long periods of prayer in small groups, praying Scripture saturated prayers, grieving over personal sin, confessing, repenting, seeking reconciliation with people. It means perseverance in prayer, not quitting until God brings it. Nothing short of revival prayer will bring revival. Are you willing to pray like that? If not, then don't expect revival. If so, then expect it, long for it, and rejoice when it comes.

---

93. Murray, *Revival and Revivalism: The Making and Marring of American Evangelicalism, 1750–1858,* 419.

94. Couper, et al, edited by Richard Owen Roberts, *Scotland Saw His Glory,* 125ff.

Bibliography

Ahlstrom, Sydney. *A Religious History of the American People*, 2 volumes. Garden City, New York: Doubleday and Company, 1975.

Andersen, Christopher. *Young Kate*. New York: Dell Publishing, 1988.

Applegate, Debby. *The Most Famous Man in America: The Biography of Henry Ward Beecher*. New York: Doubleday, 2006.

Barker, Juliet. *Agincourt: Henry V and the Battle that Made England*. New York, Boston: Little, Brown, and Company, 2005.

Barna Group, www.barna.org August 23, 2005.

Bateman, Steve. *Which Real Jesus: Jonathan Edwards, Benjamin Franklin, and the Early American Roots of the Current Debate*. Eugene, Oregon: Wipf and Stock Publishers, 2008.

Beale, David. "Lessons Learned From the Fall of Harvard." Bob Jones University.

Beuttler, Bill. "We Work Too Hard." *Boston Magazine*, November, 2001.

Bremer, Francis J. *John Winthrop: America's Forgotten Founding Father*. Oxford: Oxford University Press, 2003.

Brown, Steve. *A Scandalous Freedom: The Radical Nature of the Gospel*. West Monroe, Louisiana: Howard Publishing, 2004.

Buck, Pearl S. *Is There a Case for Foreign Missions?* New York: The John Day Company, 1932.

Burr, Esther. *Esther Burr's Journal*. Edited by Jeremiah James Rankin, third edition. Washington D.C.: Woodward and Lothrop, 1903.

Bush Jr., Sargent. *The Writings of Thomas Hooker: Spiritual Adventure in Two Worlds*. Madison, Wisconsin: The University of Wisconsin Press, 1980.

Calvin, John. *The Epistles of Paul the Apostle to the Galatians, Ephesians, Philippians, and Colossians*. Edited by David W. Torrance and Thomas F. Torrance. Translated by T.H.L. Parker. Grand Rapids: William B. Eerdmans Publishing Company, 1965.

Collingwood, Deryck. *Thomas Hooker, 1586-1647, Father of American Democracy*. Interlaken, NY: Heart of Lakes Publishers, 1995.

Couper, W.J. et al. *Scotland Saw His Glory: A History of Revivals in Scotland*. Compiled and edited by Richard Owen Roberts. Wheaton, Illinois: International Awakening Press, 1995.

Currid, John. *A Study Commentary on Exodus*. Webster, NY: Evangelical Press, 2001.

Dabney, R.L. *On Secular Education*. Edited by Douglas Wilson. Moscow, Idaho: Canon Press, 2001.

Davies, Samuel. *Sermons by the Reverend Samuel Davies*, 3 volumes. Morgan, Pennsylvania: Soli Deo Gloria Publishers, 1998.

Douglas, Ann. *The Feminization of American Culture*. New York: Farrar, Straus, and Giroux, 1977.

Edwards, Jonathan. *The Wrath of Almighty God: Jonathan Edwards on God's Judgment against Sinners*. Edited by Don Kistler. Morgan, Pennsylvania: Soli Deo Gloria Publishers, 1996.

Ferling, John. *John Adams, A Life*. Knoxville, Tennessee: The University of Tennessee Press, 1992.

Fraser, Antonia. *Royal Charles: Charles II and the Restoration*. New York: Alfred A. Knopf, 1979.

Gardner, Day. "More and More Black Babies Murdered Via Abortion." *The Hick Town Press*, February 29, 2008.

Gaustad, Edwin S. *Liberty of Conscience: Roger Williams in America*. Grand Rapids: William B. Eerdmans Publishing Company, 1991.

Gilpin, W. Clark. *The Millenarian Piety of Roger Williams*. Chicago and London: The University of Chicago Press, 1970.

Grant, George. *Grand Illusions: The Legacy of Planned Parenthood*. Brentwood, Tennessee: Wolgemuth & Hyatt Publishers, Inc. 1988.

Gray, Janet Glenn. *The French Huguenots: Anatomy of Courage*. Grand Rapids: Baker Books, 1992.

Hendriksen, William. *New Testament Commentary: Exposition of Galatians, Ephesians, Philippians, Colossians, and Philemon*. Grand Rapids: Baker Books, 1967.

Herman, Arthur. *How the Scots Invented the Modern World: The True Story of How Western Europe's Poorest Nation Created Our World & Everything In It*. New York: Crown Publishing, 2001.

Jenkins, Phillip. *The Next Christendom: The Coming of Global Christianity*. Oxford: Oxford University Press, 2007.

Johnson, Paul. *Intellectuals*. New York: Harper and Row Publishers, 1988.

Jones, Peter. *Capturing the Pagan Mind: Paul's Blueprint for Thinking and Living in the New Global Culture*. Nashville: Broadman and Holman Publishers, 2003.

Jude 3 Project, "Willow Creek Repents?" www.blog.christianitytoday.com 2007.

Kelly, Douglas F. *If God Already Knows, Why Pray?* Ross-shire, Scotland: Christian Focus Publications, 2001.

Knox, John. *The Reformation in Scotland*. Edinburgh: The Banner of Truth Trust. Reprint, 1982.

Lenski, R.C.H. *Commentary on the New Testament: The Interpretation of St. Paul's First and Second Epistles to the Corinthians*. Hendricksen Publishers, second edition, 2001.

———. *Commentary on the New Testament: The Interpretation of St. Paul's Epistles to the Galatians, to the Ephesians, and to the Philippians*. Hendricksen Publishers, second printing, 2006.

Lloyd-Jones, D. Martyn. *Growing in the Spirit: The Assurance of Salvation*. Edited by Christopher Catherwood. Westchester, Illinois: Crossway Books, 1989.

———. *Spiritual Depression: Its Causes and Cure*. Grand Rapids: William B. Eerdmans Publishing Company, 1965.

Lovelace, Richard. *The American Pietism of Cotton Mather*. Grand Rapids: William B. Eerdmans Publishing Company, 1979.

Lucas, Sean Michael. *Robert Lewis Dabney: A Southern Presbyterian Life*. Phillipsburg, New Jersey: P & R Publishing, 2005.

MacArthur, John. *Ashamed of the Gospel: When the Church Becomes Like the World*. Wheaton: Crossway Books, 1993.

Marsden, George. *Jonathan Edwards: A Life*. New Haven and London: Yale University, Press, 2003.

———. *Reforming Fundamentalism: Fuller Seminary and the New Evangelicalism*. Grand Rapids: William B. Eerdmans Publishing Company, 1987.

Mather, Cotton. *Magnalia Christi Americana*. Edinburgh: The Banner of Truth Trust, 1979.

McCullough, David. *John Adams*. New York: Simon and Schuster, 2001.

McGrath, Alister. *Christianity: An Introduction*. Oxford: Blackwell Publishing, 1997.

McLaren, Brian D. *The Church on the Other Side: Doing Ministry in the Postmodern Matrix*. Grand Rapids: Zondervan, 2000.

Miller, Donald. *Blue Like Jazz: Nonreligious Thought on Christian Spirituality*. Nashville: Thomas Nelson Publishers, 2003.

Morgan, Edmund S. *The Puritan Dilemma: The Story of John Winthrop*. Boston, Toronto: Little, Brown, and Company, 1958.

———. *Roger Williams: The Church and the State*. New York: Harcourt, Brace, and World, 1967.

Murray, Iain H. *Evangelicalism Divided: A Record of Crucial Change in the Years 1950 to 2000*. Edinburgh: The Banner of Truth Trust, 2000.

———. *D. Martyn Lloyd-Jones: The First Forty Years, 1899–1929*, Edinburgh: The Banner of Truth Trust, 1982.

———. *Jonathan Edwards: A New Biography*. Edinburgh: The Banner of Truth Trust, 1996.

———. *Revival and Revivalism: The Making and Marring of American Evangelicalism, 1750–1858*. Edinburgh: The Banner of Truth Trust, 1994.

O'Brien, Peter T. *The Letter to the Ephesians*. Grand Rapids: William B. Eerdmans Publishing Company, 1999.

Olyott, Stuart. *Preaching Pure and Simple*. Bryntirion, Wales: Bryntirion Press, 2005.

Osteen, Joel. *Your Best Life Now*. New York: Warner Faith Publishers, 2004.

Owen, John. *The Works of John Owen, volume 3*. Edited by William H. Goold. Edinburgh: The Banner of Truth Trust, reprint 1977.

Packer, J.I. *A Quest for Godliness: The Puritan Vision of the Christian Life*. Wheaton: Crossway Books, 1990.

Peckham, Colin and Mary. *Sounds from Heaven: The Revival on the Isle of Lewis, 1949–1952*. Ross-shire, Scotland: Christian Focus Publications, 2004.

Piper, John. *Contending for our All: Defending Truth and Treasuring Christ in the Lives of Athanasius, John Owen, and J. Gresham Machen*. Wheaton: Crossway Books, 2006.

———. *The Hidden Smile of God: The Fruit of Affliction in the Lives of John Bunyan, William Cowper, and David Brainerd*. Wheaton: Crossway Books, 2001.

———. *The Legacy of Sovereign Joy: God's Triumphant Grace in the Lives of Augustine, Luther, and Calvin*. Wheaton: Crossway Books, 2000.

Reymond, Robert L. *A New Systematic Theology of the Christian Faith*. Nashville: Thomas Nelson Publishers, 1998.

Ridderbos, Herman. *Paul: An Outline of His Theology*. Translated by John Richard de Witt. Grand Rapids: William B. Eerdmans Publishing Company, 1975.

Roberts, Richard Owen. *Repentance: The First Word of the Gospel*. Wheaton: Crossway Books, 2002.

Rusten, E. Michael and Sharon. *The One Year Book of Christian History*. Carol Stream, Illinois: Tyndale House Publishers, 2003.

Schama, Simon. *The Embarrassment of Riches: An Interpretation of Dutch Culture in the Golden Age.* New York: Random House, Inc. 1987.

Schleiermacher, Friedrich. *On Religion: Speeches to Its Cultured Despisers.* Edited by Richard Crouter. Cambridge: Cambridge University Press, 1988.

Shaw, Peter. *The Character of John Adams.* Chapel Hill: The University of North Carolina Press, 1976.

Sider, Ronald J. *The Scandal of the Evangelical Conscience: Why Are Christians Living Just Like the Rest of the World?* Grand Rapids: Baker Books, 2005.

Silverman, Kenneth. *The Life and Times of Cotton Mather.* New York: Harper and Row Publishers, 1984.

Smith, Morton. *Studies in Southern Presbyterian Theology.* Phillipsburg, New Jersey: P & R Publishing, 2004.

Stickelberger, Emanuel. *Calvin.* Translated by David Georg Gelzer. London: James Clark and Company, 1959.

Torrey, R.A. *Why God Used D.L. Moody.* Wheaton: World Wide Publications, reprint 2005.

Thomas, Geoffrey. Sermons on Mark's Gospel. On line www.alfredplacechurch.org.uk

Tyler, Bennent and Bonar, Andrew. *The Life and Labours of Asahel Nettleton.* Edinburgh: The Banner of Truth Trust, reprint 1975.

Vandergugten, S. "The Arminian Controversy and the Synod of Dort." *The Clarion,* 1989.

Walker, George Leon. *Thomas Hooker: Preacher, Founder, Democrat.* New York: Dodd, Mead, and Company, 1891.

Watson, Thomas. *All Things for Good.* Edinburgh: The Banner of Truth Trust, 1974.

Wells, David F. *Above All Earthly Pow'rs: Christ in a Postmodern World.* Grand Rapids: William B. Eerdmans Publishing Company, 2005.

————. *The Courage to be Protestant: Truth-lovers, Marketers, and Emergents in the Postmodern World.* Grand Rapids: William B. Eerdmans Publishing Company, 2008.

Westminster Confession of Faith, and Larger and Shorter Catechisms, with the Scripture Proofs at Large, Ross-shire, Scotland: The Publications Committee of the Free Presbyterian Church of Scotland, 1970.

www.islamonline.net, "U.K. Schools Deny Holocaust Lessons to Avoid Offence," April 5, 2007.